JANICE VANCLEAVE'S

Science Around the Year

John Wiley & Sons, Inc.
New York • Chichester • Weinheim • Brisbane • Singapore • Toronto

This book is printed on acid-free paper. ♾

Published by John Wiley & Sons, Inc.
Published simultaneously in Canada

Illustrations by Laurel Aiello © 2000 on pages 4, 5, 7–9, 11 bottom, 12, 13, 15–17, 19, 20, 25, 27, 28, 32, 33, 36–39, 41, 42, 45 bottom, 46–51, 53, 54, 56, 61–69, 73 top, 75 bottom, 76, 77, 79 insert, 80, 81, 84, 85, 88–90, 93, 95–97, 103 top, 104–107, and 109–113; © 1999 on pages 43, 45 top, 52, 55, 57, 92, 98, and 99; © 1998 on page 108; © 1997 on pages 22, 23, 35, 71, and 94; © 1995 on page 11 top; © 1989 on page 101.

Design and production by Navta Associates, Inc.

Portions of this book have been reprinted from the books *Janice VanCleave's Astronomy for Every Kid, Janice VanCleave's Biology for Every Kid, Janice VanCleave's Chemistry for Every Kid, Janice VanCleave's Constellations for Every Kid, Janice VanCleave's Dinosaurs for Every Kid, Janice VanCleave's Food and Nutrition for Every Kid, Janice VanCleave's Geography for Every Kid, Janice VanCleave's Insects and Spiders, Janice VanCleave's Machines, Janice VanCleave's Physics for Every Kid, Janice VanCleave's Plants, Janice VanCleave's Play and Find Out About Bugs, Janice VanCleave's Play and Find Out about the Human Body, Janice VanCleave's Rocks and Minerals,* and *Janice VanCleave's Weather.*

Library of Congress Cataloging-in-Publication Data

VanCleave, Janice Pratt
Janice VanCleave's science around the year / VanCleave.
p. cm.
Includes index.
Summary: Presents experiments and activities in such fields as astronomy, biology, chemistry, earth science, and physics that are in some way related to one of the four seasons.
ISBN 0-471-33096-5 (paper)
1. Science—Experiments—Juvenile literature. [1. Science—Experiments. 2. Seasons. 3. Experiments.] I. Title: Science around the year. II. Title.

Q164 . V442 2000
507'.8–dc21 99-053778

Printed in the United States of America

10 9 8 7 6 5 4 3 2 1

Dedication

It is a pleasure to dedicate this book to my friend and helpmate, my husband, Wade VanCleave.

Acknowledgments

I wish to express my appreciation to these science specialists for their valuable assistance by providing information or assisting me in finding it.

Members of the Central Texas Astronomical Society, including Johnny Barton, John W. McAnally, and Paul Derrick. Johnny is an officer of the club and has been an active amateur astronomer for more than 20 years. John is also on the staff of The Association of Lunar and Planetary Observers where he is acting Assistant Coordinator for Transit Timings of the Jupiter Section. Paul is the author of the "Stargazer" column in the *Waco Tribune-Herald.*

Dr. Glenn S. Orton, a Senior Research Scientist at the Jet Propulsion Laboratory of the California Institute of Technology. Glenn is an astronomer and space scientist who specializes in investigating the structure and composition of planetary atmospheres. He is best known for his research on Jupiter and Saturn. I have enjoyed exchanging ideas with Glenn about experiments for modeling astronomy experiments.

Virginia Malone, a science assessment consultant; Sally A. DeRoo, a science educator at Wayne State University, Detroit, Michigan; Holly Harris, a science educator at China Spring Intermediate, China Spring, Texas; and Robert Fanick, a chemist at Southwest Research Institute in San Antonio, Texas. These very special people have provided a great deal of valuable information, which has made this book even more understandable and fun.

A special note of gratitude to these educators who assisted by pretesting the activities and/or by providing scientific information: Holly Harris, China Spring Middle School, China Spring, Texas; Laura Roberts, St. Matthews Elementary, Louisville, Kentucky; and Anne Skrabanek, homeschooling consultant, Perry, Texas.

Contents

Introduction

This book presents fun science facts and projects that relate to the four seasons—autumn, winter, spring, and summer. In the 52 chapters, one for each week of the year, you'll find discovery experiments and activities about different science fields, including astronomy, biology, chemistry, earth science, and physics. Some of the chapters look at special days of the year, such as Groundhog Day and Thanksgiving, and other chapters refer to events of seasonal interest. Each season is highlighted with a list of **Dates to Mark on Your Calendar.** But while the book is divided into seasons, most of the experiments can be performed any time of the year and in any order.

Each chapter explains science terms in simple language that can be easily understood. The information provided is designed to teach facts, concepts, and problem-solving strategies. The scientific concepts are explained in basic terms with little complexity and can be applied to many similar situations. The main objective of the book is to present the fun of science. You are encouraged to learn through exploration and experimentation.

HOW TO USE THIS BOOK

You can start at any time of the year by picking a chapter about the season you are in, or you can just flip through the chapters for a topic that sounds interesting. Before you do any of the experiments, read them through completely. Once you've decided on an experiment to try, collect all the needed materials and follow all procedures carefully. The format for each chapter is as follows:

- **Did You Know?** A fun fact that identifies the focus of the chapter. This statement is followed by an explanation of the science behind the fact.
- **Fun Time!** A discovery experiment related to the fun fact. Each experiment includes a **Purpose,** which states the objective of the investigation; a complete list of easy-to-find **Materials;** a step-by-step **Procedure;** a section identifying the expected **Results;** and a **Why?** section that explains why the experiment works.
- **More Fun with . . . !** An additional fun activity relating to the topic.
- **Book List** A list of other books about the topic, both fiction and nonfiction.

GENERAL INSTRUCTIONS FOR THE EXPERIMENTS

1. Read the experiments completely before starting.
2. Collect supplies. You will have less frustration and more fun if all the materials necessary for the activity are ready before you start. You lose your train of thought when you have to stop and search for supplies. Ask an adult for advice before substituting any materials.
3. Do not rush. Follow each step very carefully; never skip steps, and do not add your own. Safety is of the utmost importance, and by reading each experiment before starting, then following the instructions exactly, you can feel confident that no unexpected results will occur.
4. Observe. If your results are not the same as those described in the experiment, carefully reread the instructions and start over from step 1.

Autumn

Autumn is a wonderful time to explore science. Autumn's cooler temperatures cause leaves to change beautiful colors and fall. September is a good time to look for monarch butterflies. Autumn is also a time to pick pumpkins and carve them into jack-o'-lanterns. At the close of the season, you can study certain animals and try to predict the length of the coming winter.

DATES TO MARK ON YOUR CALENDAR

- *September 22, 1791,* is the birth date of Michael Faraday, the British physicist known for his work in electricity and magnetism.
- *On or about September 23* is the **autumnal equinox,** a day when day and night are of equal length, marking the first day of autumn.
- *September 26, 1774,* is the birth date of Johnny Appleseed, a man famous for planting apple trees across the Midwest.
- *Columbus Day,* in honor of the famous explorer Christopher Columbus, is celebrated on the second Monday in October.
- *October 16 to 27* is a good time to look for shooting stars from the Orionid meteor shower. October 22 is probably the best night to observe (unless it's cloudy).
- *From October 20 to November 30,* look for shooting stars again, this time from the Taurid meteor shower. November 5 is perhaps the best night to observe.
- *October 24, 1632,* is the birth date of Antonie van Leeuwenhoek, a Dutch businessman who was the first to observe single cell organisms with a simple microscope.
- *October 25, 1888,* is the birth date of Admiral Richard E. Byrd, an aviator and an Arctic and Antarctic explorer.
- *Daylight saving time (DST)* ends on the last Sunday in October. Don't forget to reset your clock the night before.
- *November 9, 1731,* is the birth date of Benjamin Banneker, an African American inventor who used a clock he made to measure the movement of the stars.
- *November 15 to 20,* look for the shooting stars of the Leonid meteor shower. November 17 is the best night to view.
- Thanksgiving is the last Thursday in November.

1

Falling Leaves

DID YOU KNOW?

City lights trick trees into keeping their leaves longer!

A **deciduous** tree is one that loses its leaves in autumn. A deciduous tree's leaves are made of a **blade** (broad part) and a **petiole** (stalk). The petiole is widest at its base, where it attaches to the stem of the plant on which it grows. The layer of **cells** (basic building blocks of living things) holding the petiole to the stem is called the **abscission layer.** These cells have thin walls. Running through the petiole are tubes carrying sap into and out of the leaf. (**Sap** is a watery liquid in plants that contains **nutrients,** materials needed by living things for growth, energy, and good health.) In autumn, the cells of the abscission layer of deciduous trees produce chemicals that **digest** (break down by a chemical change) the cell walls holding the layer together. Only the transport tubes are left holding the leaf to the plant stem. The weight of the leaf, with the help of wind, causes the tubes to break, and the leaf falls. But before the leaf falls, a cork layer forms a protective scar on the stem where the petiole was attached.

While the autumn generally has cooler temperatures, it is the decrease in light that triggers the production of cell-digesting chemicals. On or about September 23 is the autumnal equinox, with equal lengths of daylight and darkness. After this date the daylight period decreases each day until on or about December 22, the **winter solstice,** the day with the shortest daylight period of the year. Because trees growing near city lights receive extra light on short autumn days, they may keep their leaves longer than other, similar trees receiving only sunlight.

FUN TIME!

Purpose

To demonstrate that a leaf's death is not what causes it to fall from the stem.

Materials

sprig with 4 or more green leaves attached
vase

Procedure

1. With adult permission, break a sprig with 4 or more green leaves attached off a bush or tree.
2. Stand the sprig in the vase.
3. Set the vase where the sprig can be observed but not disturbed for 4 weeks or more.

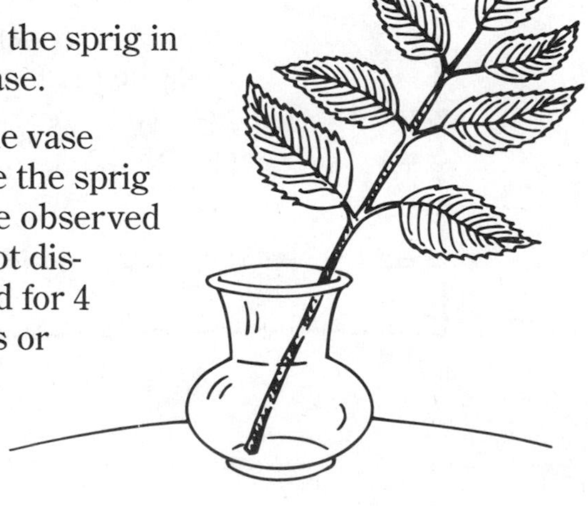

4. Observe the leaves as often as possible, but do not touch them.

Results

The green leaves die and turn brown, but do not fall off the stem.

Why?

Chemicals have not digested the walls of the cells in the abscission layer. So the cells in the abscission layer, as well as the tubes in the petiole, remain attached to the stem even after the leaf dies.

BOOK LIST

Chapman, Gillian. *Art from Wood.* Boston: Thomson Learning, 1995. Projects using branches, leaves, seeds, and other found objects.

Diehn, Gwen, and Terry Krautwurts. *Nature Crafts for Kids.* New York: Sterling, 1992. Fifty fantastic things to make with Mother Nature's help, including ways to preserve leaves.

Milford, Susan. *The Kids' Nature Book.* Charlotte, Vermont: Williamson Publishing, 1996. Indoor and outdoor nature activities for every day of the year.

VanCleave, Janice. *Plants.* New York: Wiley, 1997. Experiments about leaves and other plant parts. Each chapter contains ideas that can be turned into award-winning science fair projects.

MORE FUN WITH DRYING LEAVES!

Make an attractive arrangement of dried leaves. First, collect sprigs of different plants with green leaves attached. Arrange the sprigs in a vase like an arrangement of flowers. You can also collect dried twigs and vines without leaves and color them with acrylic paints. When the paint dries, add the colored twigs and vines to your leaf arrangement. The color of your arrangement changes over time, from spring green to brown autumnal colors.

2

Changing Colors

DID YOU KNOW?

Autumn leaves have a "sweet tooth"!

A leaf's color is caused by substances called **pigments** responding to visible light (light that can be seen, which is made up of all the rainbow colors of light rays). The green color in plants comes from **chlorophyll,** a pigment that **absorbs** (takes in) various light rays and **reflects** (throws back) the green rays. Some light rays are **transmitted** (passed through) by the pigment. As a deciduous tree prepares for winter, many of the **molecules** (particles made of two or more atoms) in the leaves, including chlorophyll molecules, break down and are recycled. The **atoms** (building blocks of all substances) of the chlorophyll molecules are used to make other kinds of molecules. These new molecules are stored in other parts of the tree.

When the green chlorophyll is gone, **carotene** (a yellow or orange pigment) can be seen in the leaves. Carotene molecules are more **stable** (not easily broken down) than those of chlorophyll, and thus are present after the chlorophyll is gone. The red and purple colors in autumn leaves are due to the production of **anthocyanins** (red to purple pigments). The amount of anthocyanin and carotene in autumn leaves is different for different **species** (specific types of living things) of plants and also for the same plant under different conditions. Cool temperatures increase the sugar content in leaves. A high sugar content and energy from the Sun favor the formation of anthocyanin. Thus, following a period of bright, sunny autumn days and cool nights, anthocyanins are produced and the leaves are gloriously colored with red to purple hues.

FUN TIME!

Purpose

To determine the effect of sunlight on leaf color.

Materials

scissors
sheet of black construction paper
houseplant with dark green leaves
transparent tape

Procedure

1. Cut 2 pieces of black construction paper large enough to cover one leaf of the plant.
2. Sandwich the leaf between the two pieces of paper, then tape the pieces of paper together. It is important that the leaf not receive any sunlight.
3. Wait 7 days or more. Then, uncover the leaf and observe its color.

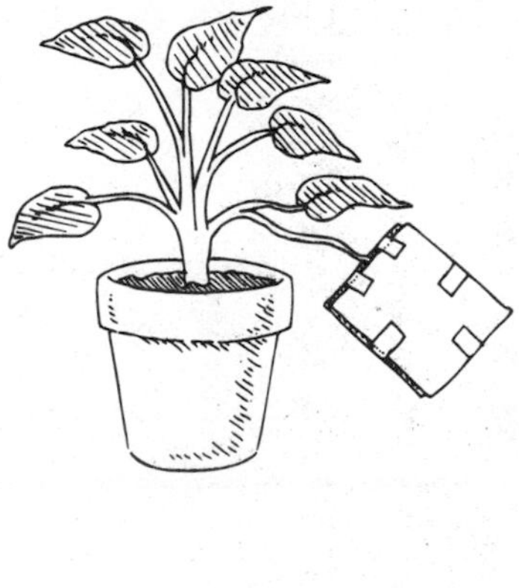

Results

The covered leaf turns from dark green to pale green or yellow.

Why?

In the absence of sunlight, green chlorophyll is not produced. The chlorophyll is used by the leaf, and because it is not replenished, the green color decreases and colors of other pigments, such as yellow carotene, can be seen.

BOOK LIST

Johnson, Sylvia A. *How Leaves Change.* Minneapolis, MN: Lerner, 1986. Describes the structure and purpose of leaves, the ways in which leaves change as part of the natural cycle of the seasons, and the process that creates their autumn colors.

Robbins, Ken. *Autumn Leaves.* New York: Scholastic, 1998. Explores the shape of leaves from different trees and explains why leaves change color.

VanCleave, Janice. *Biology for Every Kid.* New York: Wiley, 1990. Fun, simple biology experiments, including information about leaves.

———. *Plants.* New York: Wiley, 1997. Experiments about leaves and other plant parts. Each chapter contains ideas that can be turned into award-winning science fair projects.

MORE FUN WITH AUTUMN LEAVES!

Use colored autumn leaves of different shapes and sizes to make a mobile. Prepare each leaf by sandwiching it between 2 sheets of clear contact paper that is slightly larger than the leaf. Trim the paper, leaving enough near the base of each leaf to make a hole with a paper punch. Tie a string in each hole. Tie the free ends of the strings onto a clothes hanger, varying the length of the strings so that the leaves don't bump into one another and the hanger is balanced.

3

Butterfly Migration

DID YOU KNOW?

Butterflies sunbathe!

Butterflies are **cold-blooded,** which means their body temperature changes with the temperature of their surroundings. They can fly if the air temperature is 60° to 108°F (16° to 42°C), but they fly best when their body temperature is 82° to 100°F (28° to 38°C).

How can butterflies make sure that their bodies are in the ideal temperature range? They have various techniques to warm up. One way is to bask in the sun. Some sunbathe by spreading their wings and others close their wings and turn sideways to the Sun's rays. To warm their bodies before taking flight, many butterflies shiver by **vibrating** (moving quickly back and forth) their wings slightly. **Shivering** is muscle trembling. As butterflies shiver, they warm up.

When the air temperature is too hot, butterflies can cool themselves by closing their wings and turning them so that they are parallel to the sun's rays. Another method of cooling off is to fly to shady places.

When the temperature is too cold, some adult butterflies **hibernate** (live in a sleep-like condition of partial or total inactivity) and others **migrate** (move seasonally) from one region to another, often covering great distances to areas where the weather is warmer. Large numbers of monarchs fly to the southern United States and to Central America each autumn and return again in the spring. Some fly thousands of miles (km).

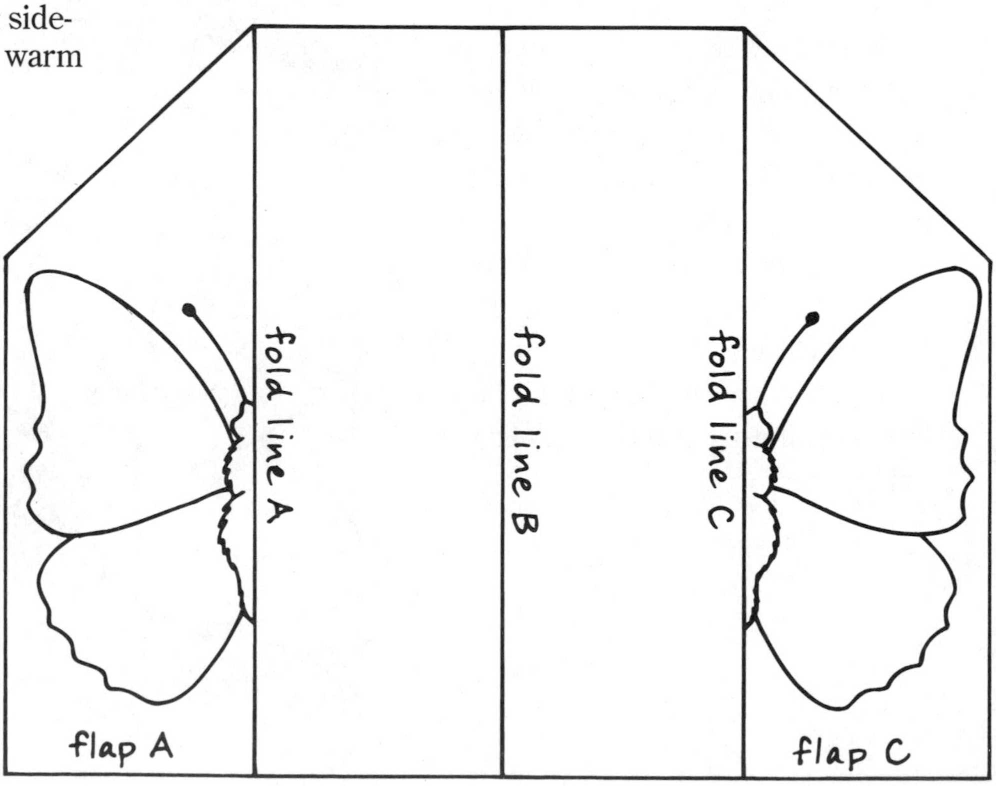

FUN TIME!

Purpose

To demonstrate how monarchs glide in flight.

Materials

sheet of unruled white paper
black marking pen
scissors
1 paper clip

Procedure

1. Lay the paper over the pattern shown on page 8 and trace all of the lines and the monarch outline. Cut out the pattern.
2. Fold the paper in half along fold line B so that the drawing is on the inside; then fold flaps A and C toward the center fold.
3. Attach the paper clip under the front end as shown.
4. Holding the paper from below (on fold line B), adjust the flaps so that they are parallel to the ground. Then throw the paper to make it glide through the air.

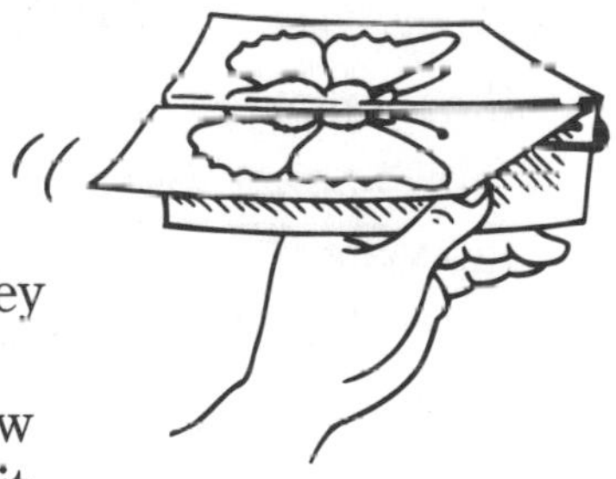

Results

The paper monarch will fly through the air, then gently glide to the ground.

Why?

Adult monarchs are great fliers, flapping slowly but strongly. Between flapping their wings, they often hold their wings open and **glide** (fly without flapping their wings) through the air. This soaring technique saves energy, allowing monarchs to fly long distances.

BOOK LIST

Carter, David. *Butterflies and Moths.* New York: Dorling Kindersley, 1992. A field guide to butterflies and moths around the world, with full-color photographs and descriptions of key features and points of differentiation.

Kneidel, Sally. *Pet Bugs.* New York: Wiley, 1994. Information about how to catch and keep touchable insects, including monarch butterflies.

Pringle, Laurence. *An Extraordinary Life.* New York: Orchard Books, 1997. Introduces the life cycle, feeding habits, migration pattern, and mating habits of the monarch butterfly through the observation of one particular monarch that the author has named Danaus.

VanCleave, Janice. *Insects and Spiders.* New York: Wiley, 1998. Experiments about butterflies and other insects as well as spiders. Each chapter contains ideas that can be turned into award-winning science fair projects.

MORE FUN WITH MONARCHS!

Most birds learn not to eat monarchs to avoid throwing up. Monarchs feed on milkweed plants, which contain chemicals that are poisonous to some animals, including birds, but are not poisonous to monarchs. When a bird eats a monarch, the milkweed chemicals in the butterfly cause the bird to throw up. Once a bird has eaten a monarch, it learns its lesson and avoids monarchs and any other butterflies with similar orange and black coloring. Color the wings of your paper monarch orange with a few white spots, then draw veins and color them black. Use a butterfly book to help you color your butterfly.

4

Johnny Appleseed

DID YOU KNOW?

One man planted hundreds of apple trees throughout the Midwest.

Around 1800, according to legend, a man with flowing hair and bare feet, wearing ragged trousers and an old coffee sack with holes cut out for his head and arms, and carrying a Bible, traveled alone from western Pennsylvania through Ohio, Indiana, and Illinois, planting apple trees. For more than 40 years this man planted, tended, and helped others plant apple orchards. The seeds and **saplings** (small trees) he planted, as well as those he gave away to settlers and Native Americans, helped to build the apple orchards of the Midwest. He became known as "Johnny Appleseed."

This man became a folk hero, and many stories were told about him after his death. Some of the stories about his appearance and deeds are true, but many may be imaginary. It is known that his real name was John Chapman, and it is thought that he was born on September 26, 1774, in Leominster, Massachusetts. He died in March 1845, in northern Indiana. He was a **nurseryman** (a person who grows and sells plants) before leaving on his apple planting journey, and it is thought that he intended to make a living from his apple orchards. He owned about 1,200 acres (490 ha) of orchards at the time of his death.

While he is best known for planting apple seeds, he also planted the seeds of many healing herbs—catnip, horehound, and pennyroyal. Despite his "hippie-like" appearance, he was regarded as a healer, and even something of a saint, by settlers and Indians alike. He is buried in Fort Wayne, Indiana, which is also the site of the annual Johnny Appleseed Festival celebrated each autumn.

FUN TIME!

Purpose

To discover how you sense an apple's taste.

Materials

3 fruit juices—apple, grape, and orange
four 3-ounce (90-ml) paper cups
tap water
scarf that can be used as a blindfold
helper

Procedure

NOTE: Do not let your helper see the juices before the experiment starts.

1. Pour each fruit juice into a cup.
2. Fill the fourth cup with water.
3. Use the scarf to blindfold your helper. Ask your helper to hold his or her nose during the experiment.
4. Hand one cup of juice to your helper and ask him or her to drink the juice and tell you if it is apple juice.

5. Have your helper drink some water to wash out the taste of the juice.
6. Repeat steps 5 and 6 for the other two juices.
7. Ask your helper to stop holding his or her nose and repeat the procedure for all three juices.

Results

When your helper is holding his or her nose, the juices have a similar taste, so it is difficult to determine which is the apple juice. When your helper is allowed to smell the juices, the different tastes are easily recognized.

Why?

The taste of a food depends not only on the taste picked up by your tongue, but also on the smell that is detected by your nose. Your tongue can tell you whether a food tastes sweet, sour, salty, or bitter, but your nose can identify thousands of smells. Apple, grape, and orange juice have a similarly sweet taste. It is the difference in smell that makes an apple and its juice have a specific "taste."

BOOK LIST

Holland, Gini. *Johnny Appleseed.* Austin, TX: Raintree/Steck-Vaughn, 1998. Describes the life and accomplishments of John Chapman.

Lawler, Laurie. *The Real Johnny Appleseed.* Albert Whitman, 1995. A study of John Chapman based on land records, census data, and local history.

Parker, Steve. *Touch, Taste, and Smell.* New York: Franklin Watts, 1982. A look at the parts of your body with which you touch, taste, and smell.

VanCleave, Janice. *Geometry for Every Kid.* New York: Wiley, 1994. Fun, simple geometry experiments, including information about symmetry.

MORE FUN WITH APPLES!

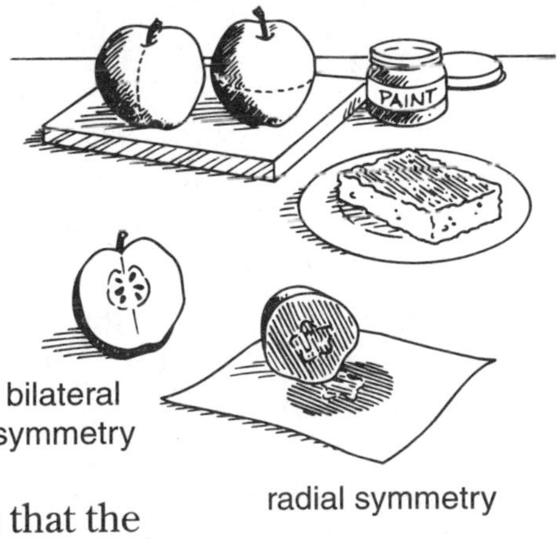

Apples have both bilateral and radial symmetry. Here's a fun way to show what these are: Ask an adult to cut an apple in half from top (where the stem is) to bottom. The two inside surfaces have **bilateral symmetry.** This means that the designs of the two halves are mirror images of each other. Ask the adult to cut a second apple in half across the middle. The inside surfaces of these two halves represent **radial symmetry.** This means that the design on each surface spreads out from the center like the spokes of a wheel.

Use the apple halves to make prints on paper. Do this by wetting a sponge with paint. Press the cut surface of one of the apples in the paint on the sponge, then press it against a sheet of paper. Repeat the procedure using an apple piece with the other kind of symmetry. The radial design has a five-pointed star shape.

5

Columbus

DID YOU KNOW?

Columbus at times had to guess where he was going when he sailed across the Atlantic!

In 1492, Christopher Columbus (1451–1506) set out across the Atlantic Ocean to find a westward route to Asia. Columbus had a few instruments to help him determine his **latitude** (angular distance north or south of an imaginary line around Earth at 0° latitude called the **equator**).

But like other sailors at that time, Columbus had no way of determining his exact **longitude** (angular distance east or west of an imaginary line around Earth at 0° longitude called the **prime meridian**). He had to guess his longitude by the distance in miles he determined he had gone from a known point. This was very inaccurate, and to prevent the ships from running aground unexpectedly, he gave orders not to travel at night when he thought the ships were close to land.

Columbus's instruments pointed out the direction of the **magnetic north pole** (the northernmost place on Earth to which a compass needle points), and **Polaris** (the North Star) pointed out the direction of true north. **True north** is the direction of the **North Pole** (north end of Earth's **axis**—imaginary line through Earth perpendicular to the equator). On his first voyage to the New World, Columbus discovered that the relation of magnetic north to true north changes with the location of the observer.

FUN TIME!

Purpose

To compare magnetic north to true north from points along the route of Columbus's first voyage.

Materials

two 16-inch (40-cm) pieces of string
globe on stand
transparent tape

Procedure

1. Make a loop in the end of one string so that it wraps around the north axis of the globe.
2. Find the magnetic north pole, at about latitude 78°N and longitude 104°W. A dot marks this spot on many globes. Tape one end of the second string to the dot (or where the dot would be).

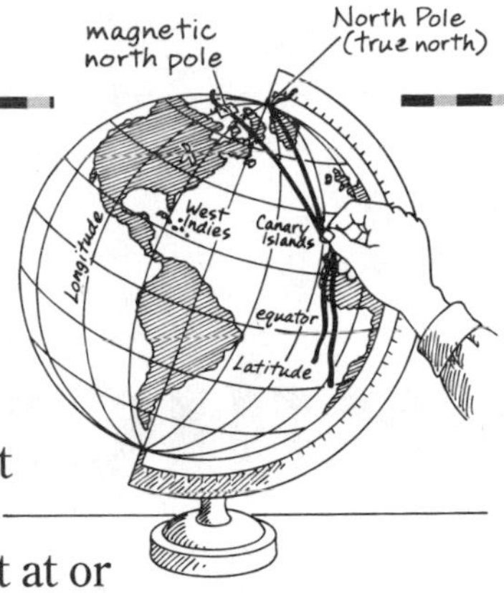

3. Using the map of Columbus's first voyage shown on page 12, pull the free ends of the two strings so that they come together at a point at or near the beginning of the voyage, such as the Canary Islands. Observe the angle between the two strings.
4. Repeat step 3 at San Salvador.

Results

When you move both strings from the point at the beginning of Columbus's voyage to the point at San Salvador, you will see that the angle between the string decreases.

Why?

The two strings point to two different places on Earth. The first points to true north, which is the North Pole, located at latitude 90°N and where all the longitude lines cross. The second string points to magnetic north, which is located at about latitude 78°N and longitude 104°W. Like you, Columbus discovered that the difference between true north and magnetic north decreased as he traveled west, toward San Salvador.

From longitudes 104°W and 104°E, magnetic north and true north are in the same direction. Check this out for yourself.

BOOK LIST

Gleiter, Jan. *Christopher Columbus.* Austin, TX: Raintree/Steck-Vaughn, 1996. Presents Columbus's life and how he came to discover the New World.

Sobel, Dava. *Longitude.* New York: Walker, 1995. The true story of John Harrison, who solved the greatest navigational problem of his time—how to find longitude.

VanCleave, Janice. *Constellations for Every Kid.* New York: Wiley, 1997. Fun, simple constellation experiments, including information about different seasonal constellations as well as star maps for each season.

———. *Geography for Every Kid.* New York: Wiley, 1993. Fun, simple geography experiments, including information about mapping and other geography skills.

MORE FUN WITH MAGNETIC NORTH AND TRUE NORTH!

Compare the difference between magnetic north and true north where you live. On a clear, moonless night, stand outdoors facing north. Find the group of stars known as the Big Dipper. (See chapter 32, "The Big Dipper," for more information.) Follow an imaginary line upward from the two outer stars in the bowl of the Big Dipper to Polaris. Lay a clipboard with a sheet of paper on the ground. Using an astronomer's flashlight (see chapter 10, "Night Vision") to see, draw a dot in the center of the paper. Draw an arrow from the dot on the paper toward a point on the horizon below Polaris. Label the head of the arrow TN for true north. Center a compass over the dot. From the edge of the compass, draw an arrow on the paper in the direction the compass needle points. Label the head of the arrow MN for magnetic north. Remove the compass and connect the end of this arrow to the dot. Observe the angle between the two lines on the paper.

6

Plant Weather Predictors

DID YOU KNOW?

Pinecones can tell you something about the weather!

An instrument that measures **humidity** (the amount of moisture in the air) is called a **hygrometer.** This instrument works because it is **hygroscopic** (absorbing water from the air). Your hair is hygroscopic. Parts of the hair strand absorb water and get fatter. This makes the hair twist and bend in different directions. So your hair is a natural hygrometer.

Pinecones are another natural hygrometer. When the seeds of a pinecone have developed, the scales of the pinecone open slightly and the seeds fall out. But the scales close when the air is very humid.

FUN TIME!

Purpose

To use a pinecone to determine humidity.

Materials

- large bowl
- tap water
- 4 to 6 mature pinecones
- timer
- cake pan
- aluminum foil
- oven
- adult helper

Procedure

1. Fill the bowl with water, and place the pinecones in the water.
2. After 30 to 45 minutes, remove the pinecones and observe their scales.
3. Line the cake pan with aluminum foil to protect the pan, and place the pinecones in the pan.
4. Have an adult helper place the pan in an oven set to low and bake the cones for 30 minutes. After 30 minutes, have the adult remove the pan from the oven.
5. When the pinecones have cooled, observe the position of the scales.

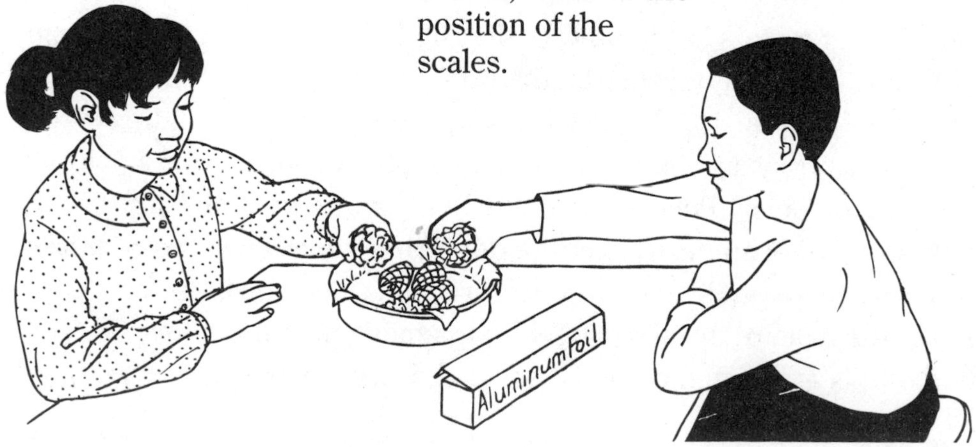

Results

When the pinecones are soaked in water, they close up. When they are dried out in the oven, they open.

Why?

Pinecones are hygroscopic. When their scales absorb water, they swell and close. Drying allows the scales to separate. Humid air has more water in it, so observing a pinecone can tell you whether the air is humid or dry.

BOOK LIST

Karl, Jonathan D. *Weather: National Audubon Society First Field Guide.* New York: Scholastic Trade, 1998. Explains what weather is, how it is measured, and how you can build your own observation devices at home.

Suzuki, David. *Looking at Weather.* New York: Wiley, 1991. Describes the changes in weather, how weather affects people's lives, and how people affect weather. Includes activities.

VanCleave, Janice. *Earth Science for Every Kid.* New York. Wiley, 1991. Fun, simple earth science experiments, including information about humidity and weather.

———. *Weather.* New York: Wiley, 1995. Experiments about humidity and other weather topics. Each chapter contains ideas that can be turned into award-winning science fair projects.

MORE FUN WITH PINECONE HYGROMETERS!

Make a pinecone hygrometer that looks like an owl to hang outdoors near your window. Use colored felt, wiggle eyes, and glue to make a large pinecone that looks like an owl as shown. Tie a string around the pinecone and hang it outdoors. If possible, hang the pinecone so that you can easily see it from indoors through a window. Observe the scales of the pinecone on different days. Your pinecone hygrometer can help you tell if it is humid or dry outside. Check its accuracy against a weather report.

7

Big Pumpkin

DID YOU KNOW?

Certain varieties of pumpkins have been known to weigh more than 1,000 pounds!

Pumpkins are a type of squash. The squash that is commonly called a pumpkin is orange, has very long vines, and has stems that are firmer, more rigid, and squarer than those of other squashes. Certain Native American tribes grew pumpkins for food long before Columbus arrived. Columbus carried pumpkin seeds back to Europe, but the pumpkins that grew from them were mainly used to feed pigs.

The first American settlers were not fond of pumpkins, but when food became scarce they experimented and came up with recipes. One tasty-sounding recipe called for cutting the top off and removing the seeds, stuffing the pumpkin with apples, sugar, spices, and milk, then baking it.

Pumpkins vary greatly in size. They can weigh less than 1 pound (0.454 kg) or more than 1,000 pounds (454 kg). Maybe it was one of these giants that Cinderella's coach was made from.

FUN TIME!

Purpose

To determine if a pumpkin is heavier than an equal volume of water.

Materials

bowl large enough to hold the pumpkin
tap water
small pumpkin

Procedure

1. Fill the bowl about three-fourths full with water.
2. Place the pumpkin in the water, and observe the pumpkin.

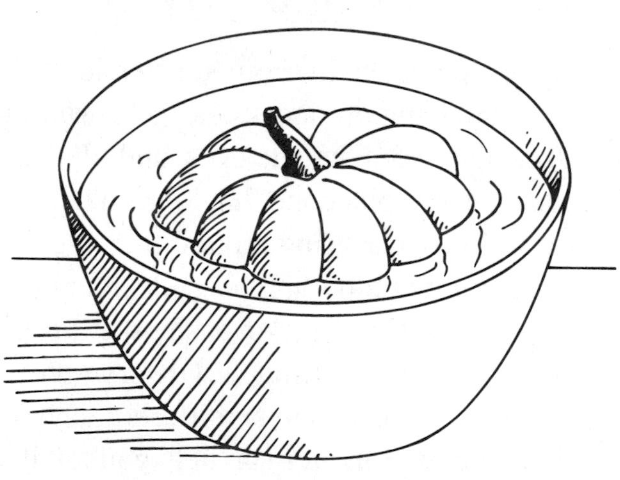

Results

The pumpkin floats in the water.

Why?

No matter how large a pumpkin is, it will float if placed in enough water. This is because the larger the pumpkin, the larger its hollow center.

This makes its density less than the density of water. **Density** is a measure of the **mass** (an amount of material) of a given **volume** (amount of space occupied) of a material. A volume of water equal to the volume of the pumpkin has more mass than the pumpkin, so the pumpkin floats.

BOOK LIST

Kite, Patricia L. *Gardening Wizadry for Kids.* Hauppauge, NY: Barron's, 1995. History and folklore of common fruits and vegetables and gardening activities.

VanCleave, Janice. *Plants.* New York: Wiley, 1997. Experiments about seeds and other plant parts. Each chapter contains ideas that can be turned into award-winning science fair projects.

MORE FUN WITH PUMPKINS!

Your pumpkin is filled with seeds. If you have an outdoor garden, you may wish to plant the seeds and grow your own pumpkins. If so, ask an adult to cut the top off the pumpkin so that you can use a spoon or your hands to scoop out the seeds. Rinse the seeds in water, lay them on a paper towel to air dry, then store the dry seeds in a resealable bag until you are ready to plant them. In early spring, purchase a package of pumpkin seeds at the store and follow the instructions for the best planting time in your area. Plant a few of the store-bought seeds and the ones you collected from your pumpkin. Compare the size of the pumpkins grown from both seeds.

Use your hollowed-out pumpkin to make a jack-o'-lantern. With adult supervision, use pumpkin-carving tools to cut a face in your pumpkin. Ask permission to place a candle inside your jack-o'-lantern so that its face glows.

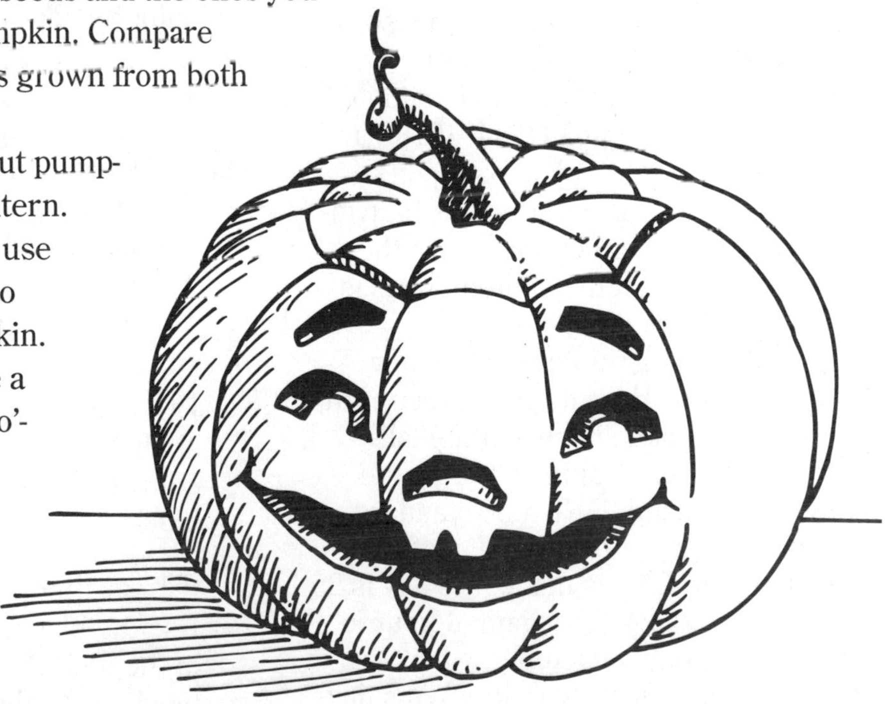

8

Saving Time

DID YOU KNOW?

One day of the year is 23 hours long!

Daylight saving time (DST) in the United States falls between the first Sunday of April and the last Sunday of October. In April clocks are set forward 1 hour, and in October they are set back 1 hour. Here are two ways to remember which way to set your clocks:

- In the spring, the time springs forward 1 hour.
- In the fall, the time falls back 1 hour.

People invented daylight saving time so that they would have more usable hours of daylight in the evening. Great Britain adopted this plan during World War I (1914–1918), and the United States used the plan for the first time after World War I. But until 1966, individual states or cities had the option to use the plan or not. Now most of the United States is on DST between April and October.

The amount of daylight doesn't actually change (although the days do get longer in the spring and summer and shorter in the fall—see chapter 30, "Spring Equinox"), only the time changes. So during DST, 4:00 standard time is 5:00 DST. On the first Sunday of April, when the change to DST is made, the day is 25 hours long instead of 24. This gained hour is lost on the last Sunday of October, when clocks are set back to standard time. This day is 23 hours long.

FUN TIME!

Purpose

To compare sun time and clock time.

Materials

hammer
3-inch (7.5-cm) 16d nail or other long nail
2-by-4-by-6-inch (5-by-10-by-15-cm) wooden block
watch
2 markers—1 black, 1 red
adult helper

Procedure

1. Ask your adult helper to hammer the tip of the nail near one end of the wooden block. The nail should be as firm and vertical as possible without being driven in too deeply. This is your sun clock.
2. On a sunny day during the week before DST ends, take the sun clock outdoors about 5 minutes before 10 o'clock (or any convenient hour). Note the direction of the block.
3. Set the sun clock in a sunny area.
4. Use the black marker to trace the shadow of the nail where it falls across the wooden block. Note the time on your watch and write it on the shadow line.

5. Using the red marker, repeat steps 3 and 4 at 9 o'clock (or 1 hour earlier) on a sunny day during the first week of standard time—after DST ends. (Be sure to remember to set your watch back 1 hour and place the block in the same direction as before.)
6. Compare the shadow lines and the clock times.

Results

The shadow lines are close to each other or overlapping, but the clock times are different by 1 hour.

Why?

The sun clock shows that although clock time changes after daylight saving time ends, the time by the sun doesn't.

BOOK LIST

Gibbin, Mary. *Eyewitness Science: Time and Space.* New York: Dorling Kindersley, 1995. A book about time and space that includes measuring time.

VanCleave, Janice. *Math for Every Kid.* New York: Wiley, 1991. Fun, simple math experiments, including information about time.

Walpole, Brenda. *Time.* Milwaukee, WI: Gareth Stevens, 1995. Explains time and various ways to measure it, from shadow clocks and digital watches to calendars and time zones.

MORE FUN WITH TIME!

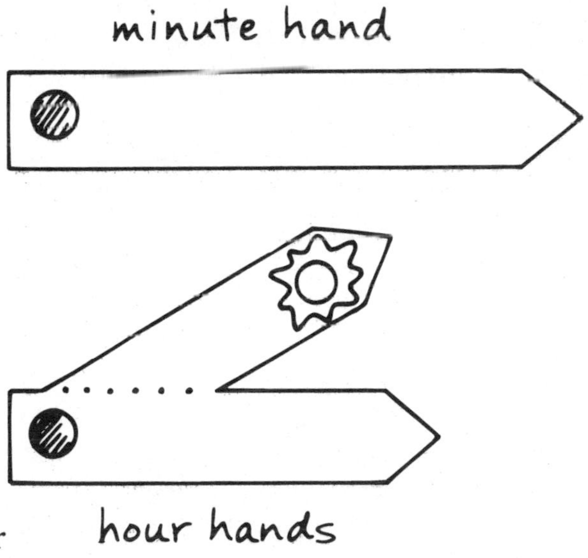

A fun clock can be made to show the difference between DST and standard time, or sun time. First, draw a 6-inch (15-cm)-diameter circle on stiff paper, such as poster board. Cutout the circle and draw a clock face on it. Trace the minute and hour hands of the clock shown here and glue them to stiff paper. Cut out the hands, keeping the two hour hands stuck together.

Using a paper punch, make a hole in the ends of each hand. Use a paper brad to secure the hands to the center of the clock face. Turn the minute hand so that it points to 12. Before DST ends, turn the hour hands so that the plain hand points to clock time, or DST. The hour hand with the sun figure will show sun time, or standard time.

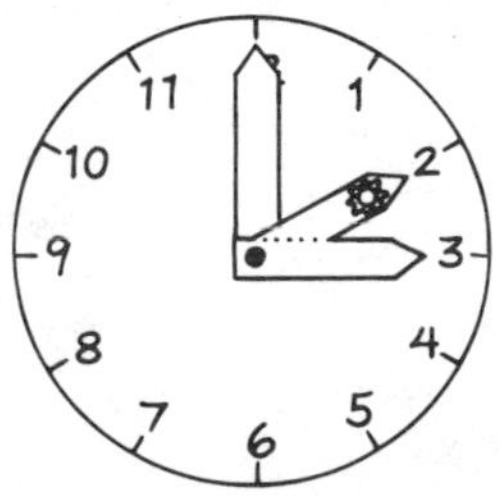

9

Cleaning Up

DID YOU KNOW?

You can do a first-class job raking leaves with a third-class lever!

In autumn, people use rakes to gather fallen leaves. A rake is an example of a type of machine called a lever. **Levers** include bars, boards, or straight sticks that rotate about a fixed point, the **fulcrum.** When you use a rake, you put one of your hands above the other. The fulcrum is the point where your upper hand holds the rake handle. You move the rake by pushing or pulling with your lower hand. You apply an **effort force** (the force applied to the lever) on the rake. The teeth of the rake apply a **resistance force** (the force the lever applies) on the **load,** which is the object being moved, the leaves.

There are three classes (kinds) of levers based on the position of the effort force, resistance force, and fulcrum. In a **first-class lever,** such as a seesaw, the fulcrum is between the effort and resistance forces. In a **second-class lever,** such as a wheelbarrow, the resistance force is between the effort force and the fulcrum. For a **third-class lever,** such as a rake, the effort force is between the fulcrum and the resistance force.

FUN TIME!

Purpose

To demonstrate the advantage of using a third-class lever.

Materials

12 sheets of paper (used notebook paper is good)
broom
timer
helper

Procedure

1. Crumple the sheets of paper into fist-size wads.
2. Place 2 crumpled sheets together on the floor.
3. At a distance of two steps away or more, place 2 more crumpled sheets on the floor.
4. Repeat step 3 four times, randomly placing pairs of crumpled sheets around on the floor.
5. Once the pairs are distributed, ask your helper to time you as you walk around collecting 1 sheet from each pair, placing them in a pile on the floor. Record the time it took to collect the sheets into a pile.

6. Again ask your helper to time you as you use the broom to sweep the remaining sheets into the pile with the other sheets.
7. Compare the time it took to collect the sheets by hand to the time it took to sweep them.

Results

It took longer to collect the crumpled sheets by hand than to sweep them into a pile.

Why?

A broom, like a rake, is a third-class lever. The broom allows you to reach out and move objects (the crumpled sheets) instead of having to walk to each object and bend over to pick it up. Another advantage of the broom and the rake is that the straw and teeth spread out wide so that they can cover a large area and sweep up more objects at one time than your hand can. Not only did the broom save time, but less effort was needed to use the broom than to bend and pick up the crumpled sheets one at a time.

BOOK LIST

Oxlade, Chris. *Science Magic with Machines.* Hauppauge, NY: Barron's, 1995. Ten magic tricks using machines, including a mystery box that makes objects disappear and a wand that gives magicians super strength.

VanCleave, Janice. *Machines.* New York: Wiley, 1993. Experiments about levers and other machines. Each chapter contains ideas that can be turned into award-winning science fair projects.

Wells, Robert E. *How Do You Lift a Lion?* Morton Grove, IL: Albert Whitman, 1996. A fun way to learn the functions of simple machines, such as levers, wheels, and pulleys. You'll discover how to lift a lion, pull a panda, and deliver a basket of bananas to a baboon birthday party.

MORE FUN WITH LEVERS!

Play a game using a third-class lever. Make the lever by tying one end of a 3-foot (1-m) string to one end of a yardstick (meterstick). Tie the free end of the string to a metal screw ring of a 1-quart (1-liter) canning jar. Any metal ring with a diameter of about 2½ inches (6.4 cm) will work. Stand a short-necked bottle on the floor. If the bottle is plastic, fill it with water and seal with a lid, so it is heavy and not easily turned over. As in the drawing, wrap one hand around the measuring stick as close to the free end as possible. This hand is hand 1. Place hand 2 in front of hand 1 in the same way you would hold a baseball bat. Stand so that the metal ring dangles directly above the top of the bottle. Try to hook the ring over the mouth of the bottle by moving the measuring stick only with hand 2, keeping both hands near the end of the stick. Determine how many tries it takes to hook the bottle. Once you have hooked the bottle, or if you are not successful in 10 tries, let someone else attempt to hook it and break your record.

Autumn

10

Night Vision

DID YOU KNOW?

Eating an orange can help you see the stars!

The substances in the **retina** (inner, light-sensitive lining at the back of the eyeball) that detect light are called **photosensitive pigments.** The main photosensitive pigment in the eye is called **visual purple,** and it is composed of two parts: a protein molecule, and a molecule made from vitamin A. People who have a deficiency of vitamin A cannot make enough visual purple to see well at night. This condition is called **night blindness.**

Use of vitamin A tablets or eating a diet rich in foods containing vitamin A, such as fish-liver oil and butter, can help restore night vision lost due to vitamin A deficiency. So can eating some fruits and vegetables, such as oranges, tangerines, pumpkins, carrots, and bananas, which do not contain vitamin A, but do contain an orange pigment called carotene, which can be changed by your liver to vitamin A. *CAUTION: Vitamin supplements should be taken only with your physician's approval.*

FUN TIME!

Purpose

To construct and test an astronomer's flashlight.

Materials

- scissors
- ruler
- red transparent report folder
- flashlight
- rubber band
- star map

Procedure

1. Cut a 4-by-8-inch (10-by-20-cm) strip from the red folder.
2. Fold the strip in half to make a 4-inch (10-cm) square.
3. Cover the end of the flashlight with the square and secure it with the rubber band.
4. On a clear, moonless night, go outside with your flashlight and a star map and observe the stars. Notice that after a while the stars appear to be brighter. This means your night vision is working.
5. Use your astronomer's flashlight to read the star map, then turn it off and again look at the stars. How long does it take before the stars appear to shine as brightly as before?

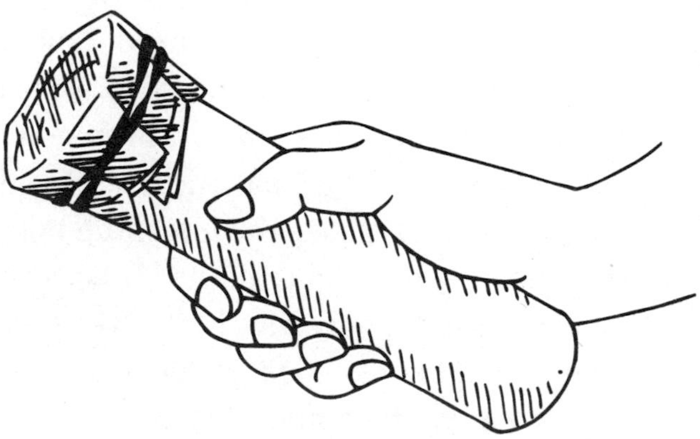

Results

An astronomer's flashlight is constructed, which can be used to read in the dark with little change in your night vision.

Why?

One way your eyes adjust to the dark is that the **pupils** (black dot–like openings in the center of your eyes) **dilate** (get bigger) to let in more light. When you go outdoors at night, it takes about 30 minutes to 1 hour for your eyes to adjust so that you can see your best in the dark. One flash of white light, such as from an uncovered flashlight, can reverse the changes in your eyes and cause you to lose your night vision. **White light** is visible light that is made up of all the rainbow colors of light. The red light in this investigation is made up mostly of red, orange, and yellow light rays, so it affects night vision less than white light. **Astronomers** (scientists who study **celestial bodies**—natural objects in the sky, such as stars, the Moon, and the Sun) cover their flashlights with a red filter, then use them to read star maps.

BOOK LIST

Levitt, I. M., and Roy K. Marshall. *Star Maps for Beginners.* New York: Simon & Schuster, 1992. Easy-to-read star maps for each month of the year.

Rey, Hans Augusto. *Find the Constellations.* New York: Houghton Mifflin, 1980. Describes stars and constellations throughout the year and the ways of identifying them.

VanCleave, Janice. *Constellations for Every Kid.* New York: Wiley, 1997. Fun, simple constellation experiments, including information about different seasonal constellations as well as star maps for each season.

———. *Astronomy for Every Kid.* New York: Wiley, 1991. Fun, simple astronomy experiments, including information about stars and other celestial bodies.

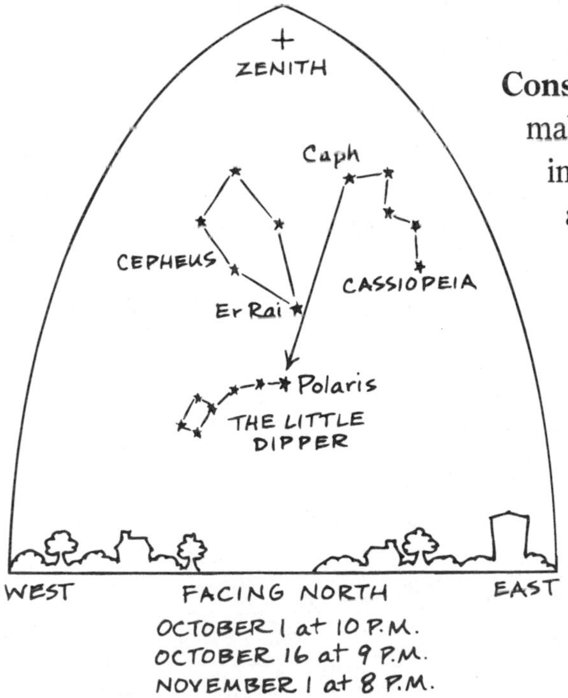

MORE FUN WITH STARS!

Constellations are groups of stars that appear to make patterns in the sky. Two constellations found in the autumn sky are the W shape of Cassiopeia and the house shape of Cepheus, both of which are upside down in autumn. Use your astronomer's flashlight and the star map shown here to find these two constellations. Stand outside facing the direction indicated at the bottom of the map—north. Hold the map in front of you so that the bottom of the map faces you. Adjust the height and angle until the map is easy to read. Note that the constellation at the bottom of the map will be found nearer the horizon you are facing. The **zenith** is the point in the sky directly overhead.

11

Static Charge

DID YOU KNOW?

Cool, dry weather can be shocking!

All **matter** is made up of atoms. Atoms have a center, called a **nucleus,** which contains positively charged particles called **protons.** Spinning outside the positively charged nucleus are negatively charged particles called **electrons.** When materials are rubbed together, electrons tend to be rubbed off one of the materials and onto the other. This causes one of the materials to be more positively charged and the other material more negatively charged. This buildup of electric charges is called **static electricity.**

For example, when your feet rub against a carpet, electrons from the carpet are rubbed onto your feet. Since opposite charges attract, as you get close to another object, especially a metal object, such as a doorknob, the protons on the object attract the extra electrons on your body. If the air is moist, the water molecules in the air bump into you and pick up the extra electrons, preventing them from collecting on your body. Cold air can hold fewer water drops than warm air. So, in autumn and winter when the air is usually cool and dry, it is easier for extra electrons to build up on your body. The movement of the electrons from your body to another object before you touch the object causes you to feel a slight shock, and if it is dark enough, you can see a spark of light.

FUN TIME!

Purpose

To demonstrate the effect of static electricity.

Materials

20 to 25 pieces of puffed-rice cereal
2-foot (60-cm) -square piece of plastic food wrap
sheet of notebook or unruled white paper

Procedure

1. Put the pieces of cereal on a table.
2. Crumple the plastic wrap into a fist-size wad.
3. Quickly rub the crumpled plastic wrap back and forth across the sheet of paper 10 to 15 times. Immediately hold the plastic above the cereal pieces, near but not touching the cereal.

Results

The cereal leaps up to the plastic.

Why?

When two substances are rubbed together, such as the plastic and the paper, electrons are lost from one substance (the paper) and gained by the other (the plastic). The electric charges that build up on an object are called **static charges** because they are stationary (nonmoving). When the negatively charged plastic approaches the cereal, the positively charged protons on the cereal are attracted to the negatively charged electrons on the plastic. This attraction is great enough for the lightweight cereal to move upward against the downward pull of **gravity** (the force that pulls things toward the center of Earth), and the cereal sticks to the plastic.

BOOK LIST

Harper, Suzanne. *Lightning: Sheets, Streaks, Beads, and Balls.* Danbury, CT: Franklin Watts, 1997. Discusses ancient legends about lightning as well as what scientists have learned about this phenomenon in recent years.

VanCleave, Janice. *Electricity.* New York: Wiley, 1994. Experiments about charged particles and other electricity-related topics. Each chapter contains ideas that can be turned into award-winning science fair projects.

———. *Molecules.* New York: Wiley, 1993. Experiments about atoms and molecules. Each chapter contains ideas that can be turned into award-winning science fair projects.

Wells, Robert E. *What's Smaller Than a Pygmy Shrew?* Morton Grove, IL: Albert Whitman, 1998. The pygmy shrew is among the smallest of mammals, but there are smaller things. In this delightful book, Wells introduces readers to all things smaller than a pygmy shrew—from ladybugs and protozoa right down to atoms and quarks!

MORE FUN WITH CHARGED PARTICLES!

Use the attraction between opposite charges to create a moving butterfly model. Draw a butterfly on a 4-inch (10-cm) -square piece of tissue paper. Cut out the butterfly design. Put a small amount of glue on the bottom of the butterfly's body, and glue it to a 6-inch (15-cm) -square piece of cardboard. Make sure the wings are not glued down. Allow the glue to dry. Crease the wings next to the body so that they bend up and down easily. Charge an inflated balloon (make sure the balloon is dry) by rubbing it on your hair. Hold the charged balloon near but not touching the wings, then move it away. Repeat this motion of the balloon to cause the butterfly wings to flutter up and down.

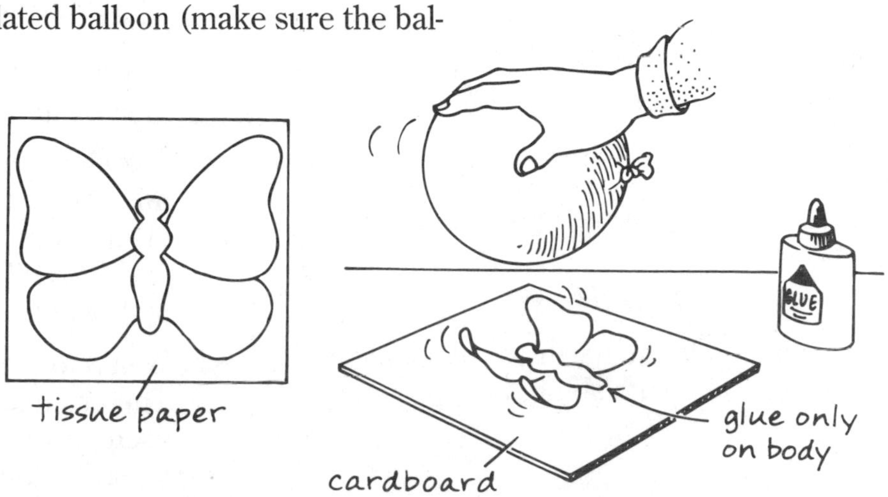

Autumn

12

Native Popcorn

DID YOU KNOW?

Native Americans may have served popcorn to the Pilgrims!

Massasoit (1580?–1661), chief of the Wampanoag, helped the Pilgrims of Plymouth Colony. He and others in his tribe taught the Pilgrims to plant native vegetables, including corn and pumpkins, and to hunt native game, such as turkeys. In 1621, the Wampanoags and the Pilgrims joined together in the first Thanksgiving ceremony to celebrate a good harvest and peace between their people. The Wampanoag brought many foods to the feast, maybe even popcorn!

The American Indians grew different kinds of corn, including yellow corn and popcorn, that are still favorite food corns, as well as varieties with red, blue, pink, and black kernels that are now used mainly for autumn decorations. Columbus and other explorers introduced corn to Europe. Corn is now grown in all parts of the world suitable to its cultivation.

FUN TIME!

Purpose

To determine how the hardness of a popcorn kernel's hull affects its ability to pop.

Materials

marker
two 3-ounce (90-ml) paper cups
20 popcorn kernels
tap water
2 paper towels
plastic food wrap
oven mitts
adult helper

Procedure

1. Use the marker to label the cups A and B. Then put 10 popcorn kernels in each cup.
2. Cover the kernels in cup B with water. Allow the kernels to soak overnight.
3. Pour the water out of cup B and place the popcorn from the cup on one of the paper towels. Blot the kernels dry with the paper towel.
4. Use the second paper towel to dry the inside of the cup. Then place the soaked popcorn kernels back into cup B.
5. Cover the top of both cups with the plastic food wrap.
6. Ask an adult to heat cups A and B in a microwave for 2 minutes and to use the oven mitts to remove the cups from the oven. *CAUTION: The cups and contents will be hot.*
7. Wait 3 to 4 minutes for the cups to cool. Then remove the plastic covering from each cup and examine the popcorn kernels in each. Compare the number of kernels that popped and the size of the popped kernels in each cup.

Results

The unsoaked popcorn in cup A popped normally. In cup B, some of the soaked kernels popped into small pieces of popped corn and others did not pop at all.

Why?

Popcorn is different from other corn in that its kernel has a very hard hull (outer covering). When heated, the water inside the kernels turns to gas. The hard hull keeps the gas from escaping, causing pressure to build up inside the kernel when heated. When the pressure is great enough, the kernel explodes and the inside material is blown out of the kernel, forming a white fluffy mass. The popped corn is about 20 to 30 times its original size. Soaking the popcorn in cup B made the hull soft. The soft hull allowed some or all of the expanding gas to leak out, resulting in small popped corn and unpopped kernels.

BOOK LIST

dePaola, Tomie. *The Popcorn Book.* New York: Harcourt Brace, 1978. Interesting facts about popcorn.

King, David C. *Colonial Days.* New York: Wiley, 1997. Kids follow a family through the year 1732 in colonial Massachusetts. Contains lots of fun activities.

Peters, Russell M. *Clambake.* Minneapolis, MN: Lerner, 1992. Steven Peters is a 12-year-old Wampanoag Indian in Massachusetts. Steve's grandfather teaches him how to prepare a clambake in the tradition of their people.

San Souci, Robert. *N. C. Wyeth's Pilgrims.* San Francisco: Chronicle Books, 1991. This beautifully illustrated book recounts the coming of the Pilgrims to America and the first Thanksgiving.

VanCleave, Janice. *Chemistry for Every Kid.* New York: Wiley, 1989. Fun, simple chemistry experiments, including information about gases.

MORE FUN WITH POPCORN!

Popcorn was used by the American Indians not only for food but for religious ceremonies and decorations. To make popcorn decorations, use a threaded needle to string popped corn. You can also add beads at different places along the string to form patterns. Short strands of popcorn and beads can be used to decorate your Thanksgiving table. Long strands can decorate a Christmas tree.

13

Animal Weather Predictors

DID YOU KNOW?

Some people think animals can predict the weather!

Weather legends or lore are ideas about weather forecasting that are passed from one generation to the next. Some of these beliefs are reliable, such as the belief that the number of chirps a cricket makes increases as the temperature increases, but many are not.

One animal that some people think can predict the weather is the woolly bear, which is the caterpillar of the tiger moth. This creepy-crawly has a band of brown hair around the middle of its body and black bands of hair on each end. The wider the brown band, the milder the winter. Other people believe that the thicker the fur of animals at the end of autumn, the more severe the winter will be.

Probably the best-known animal weather legend is that a groundhog can predict the length of winter. Each year on February 2, reporters gather in Punxsutawney, Pennsylvania, with cameras focused on the burrow of a groundhog called Punxsutawney Phil. It is said that if Phil wakes from his winter nap, sticks his head out of his burrow, and sees his shadow, he will be frightened and return to his bed and sleep for another 6 weeks. This means that winter will last another 6 weeks. If Phil doesn't see his shadow, he remains outdoors, signaling an early spring.

Woolly Bear

Are Phil and other animals reliable forecasters? Most scientists think not, but why not test them yourself?

FUN TIME!

Purpose

To test the reliability of different animal weather lore.

Animal Weather Lore

Animal	Date	Observation	Weather Prediction	Actual Weather
Woolly bear				
Dog				
Groundhog				

Materials

ruler
pen
sheet of unruled white paper

Procedure

1. Using the ruler, pen, and paper, prepare a table similar to the one shown on page 28.
2. Collect the following information and record it in the Observation column of the table:
   - Woolly bears—width of brown band
   - Dog—thickness of fur
   - Groundhog—visibility of shadow (Check a TV news program on February 2.)
3. Make a weather prediction based on your observation and the animal lore you know. Record it in the Weather Prediction column of the table.
4. When winter is over, record the actual weather in the final column. Were your predictions correct?

Results

Results will vary.

Why?

You cannot conclusively decide about the reliability of the prediction of animals you tested after just one test. After all, even **meteorologists** (scientists who study the weather) using modern equipment aren't accurate 100 percent of the time. Try again next year and see if the results are the same.

BOOK LIST

Christian, Spencer. *Can It Really Rain Frogs?* New York: Wiley, 1997. Information about the weather, including animal weather lore.

VanCleave, Janice. *Weather.* New York: Wiley, 1995. Experiments about the weather. Each chapter contains ideas that can be turned into award-winning science fair projects.

MORE FUN WITH ANIMALS!

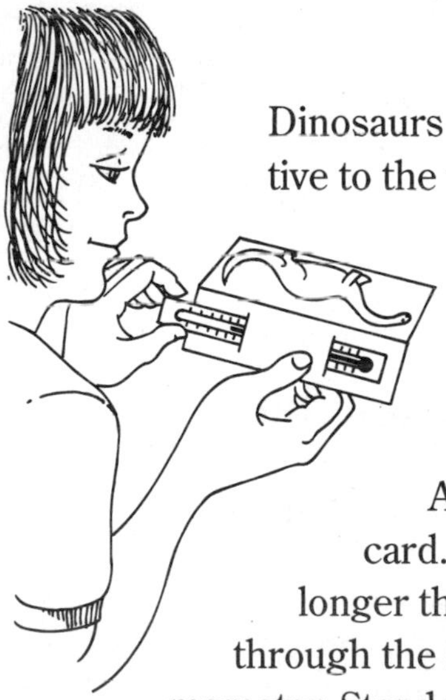

Dinosaurs were cold-blooded animals, and as such were particularly sensitive to the weather. If you could observe a dinosaur, the dinosaur's behavior would give you a clue to the outdoor temperature. Where would the dinosaur be if the outdoor temperature was very hot? Very cold?

To model your prediction, fold an unruled index card in half lengthwise. Draw a dinosaur on one side of the folded card. Ask an adult to cut two slits in the center of the other side of the card. The slits should be about 2 inches (5 cm) apart and slightly longer than the width of an outdoor thermometer. Insert the thermometer through the slits in the card. Read and record the temperature on the thermometer. Stand the dinosaur card outdoors so that the thermometer is in direct sunlight. After 5 minutes, read and record the temperature. Stand the dinosaur card in a shady area for 5 minutes. Read and record the temperature. Compare the readings.

Winter

Winter is a time of cold temperatures and, in some places, ice and snow. Besides being a fun time to study the shapes of snow crystals, winter is a great time to observe celestial bodies because the sky is generally clearer. Look for colored rainbows around the moon and find some of the many constellations visible in winter, including Orion the Hunter and Ursa Major, the Great Bear, where the Big Dipper is located.

DATES TO MARK ON YOUR CALENDAR

- *December 7 to 15* is a good time to look for shooting stars from the Geminid meteor shower, with December 13 probably being the best night to observe.
- *December 14, 1911,* is the date that Norwegian Roald Amundsen and his men became the first explorers to reach the South Pole on foot.
- *On or about December 22* is the winter solstice, the first day of winter and the shortest day of the year.
- *December 27, 1822,* is the birth date of Louis Pasteur, the French chemist who discovered that many diseases are caused by germs.
- *January 7, 1610,* is the date that Galileo Galilei discovered the moons of Jupiter. You too can see the moons of Jupiter with even a low-powered telescope.
- *February 2* is Groundhog Day.
- *February 11, 1847,* is the birth date of Thomas Alva Edison, the American inventor.
- *February 14* is Valentine's Day.
- *February 15, 1564,* is the birth date of Galileo, the Italian astronomer who made the telescope famous. But he wasn't the first to use one. Hans Lippershey (1570–1619), a Dutch spectacle maker, is given credit for the invention of the telescope in 1608.

14

Melting Ice

DID YOU KNOW?

Salt will melt ice, but sand won't!

In wintertime, both salt and sand are used to keep cars from slipping on icy roads and people from slipping on icy sidewalks. Only one of these materials actually melts ice, however. When water **freezes** (changes from a liquid to a solid due to a decrease in temperature), the molecules combine to form **ice crystals.** (**Crystals** are solid materials with flat surfaces and particles arranged in repeating patterns.) These crystals then join together in a solid block. Because the molecules on the surface of ice aren't joined to anything above, they move back and forth more easily and are more liquid-like than the molecules beneath the surface. This makes the surface of ice slippery.

At near-freezing temperatures, ice is said to have a "wet" slippery surface. But at temperatures well below freezing, ice has a "dry" surface and is barely slippery at all. This is because as the ice gets colder, the surface molecules are bound together more tightly. Salt applied to an icy sidewalk will melt the ice, but the salt may damage plants along the sidewalk. This is why sand is often used to make sidewalks and roads less slippery.

FUN TIME!

Purpose

To demonstrate the effects of salt and sand on ice.

Materials

tape	½ teaspoon (2.5 ml) sand
marking pen	½ teaspoon (2.5 ml) salt
2 saucers	freezer
2 ice cubes	timer

Procedure

1. Use the tape and marker to label one saucer SALT and the other SAND.
2. Place 1 ice cube in each saucer.
3. Place the sand on the ice in the saucer marked SAND.
4. Place the salt on the ice in the saucer marked SALT.
5. Place both saucers in the freezer.
6. Observe the contents of the saucers every 10 minutes for 30 minutes or more.

Results

The ice covered with salt begins to melt, but the ice covered with sand does not melt.

Why?

When salt and water are mixed together the salt **dissolves,** which means the salt breaks into small particles that thoroughly mix with the water. A mixture of a liquid and a dissolved substance is called a **liquid solution.** A solution of salt water has a lower **freezing point** (temperature at which a substance freezes) than does water alone. The greater the **concentration** (measure of the amount of dissolved particles in a liquid) of the salt water, the lower its freezing point. So when salt is sprinkled on the surface of "wet" ice, the salt dissolves in the water-like surface layer of the ice and causes the ice to melt. Even though the solution is at or slightly below the freezing point of water, the salt water does not refreeze.

At very low temperatures, it is difficult to melt ice with salt because the ice has a dry surface and salt cannot dissolve in the tightly bound surface ice. So the ice doesn't melt.

Sand is used to create a nonslippery barrier between you and the ice. It doesn't dissolve in the ice and cause it to melt, but due to **friction** (a force that tends to stop the motion of objects that are moving against each other), sand can break the ice into tiny pieces, causing it to melt.

BOOK LIST

Potter, Jean, and K. Whelan Dery. *Science Arts.* Bellingham, WA: Bright Ring, 1993. Discovering science through art, including sand and salt activities, complete with simple instructions and illustrations. Each activity introduces and explains a scientific concept.

VanCleave, Janice. *Chemistry for Every Kid.* New York: Wiley, 1989. Fun, simple chemistry experiments, including information about the effect of salt on ice.

Wick, Walter. *A Drop of Water: A Book of Science and Wonder.* New York: Scholastic Trade, 1997. Shows the many forms of water. With the aid of stop-action photography, water is revealed as rainbows, bubbles, drops, steam, ice, and frost.

MORE FUN WITH SALT AND SAND!

You can make some icy-looking scenes with salt, sand, waxed paper, and glue. Place a sheet of waxed paper on newspaper or a tray. Draw an icy scene on the waxed paper with white glue. Sprinkle sand or salt onto the glue drawing. Use the sand where you want dark structures and the salt for icy landscapes or ice sculptures.

15

Winter Stars

DID YOU KNOW?

You can see a hunter in the winter sky!

The winter season offers many spectacular constellations, and one of them is Orion, the Hunter, of Greek legend. Alnitak, Alnilam, and Mintaka are three equally bright stars in a row from east to west that form Orion's Belt. Two other noticeable stars in the constellation are Rigel, which is at Orion's left knee, and Betelgeuse, at his right shoulder.

Orion is imagined as having a club raised high over his head in his right hand and a shield raised in his left hand to ward off an attack by Taurus, the Bull. One of the bull's eyes is marked by the star Aldebaran.

Orion has two hunting dogs: the constellations Canis Major, the Great Dog, and Canis Minor, the Little Dog. Canis Major can be found by following a line along Orion's belt southeast to Sirius, the brightest star in the sky. Sirius is commonly known as the Dog Star. You might imagine this star as a jewel on the dog's collar.

FUN TIME!

Purpose

To find the Winter Circle.

Materials

astronomer's flashlight from chapter 10

Procedure

1. On a clear, moonless night, sit in a lawn chair outdoors facing south. Hold this book in your lap so that the bottom of the star map shown on page 35 faces you.
2. Adjust the height and angle of the map so that with the flashlight, the map is easy to read.
3. Using the flashlight, look at the map to find the location of Orion. Then turn off the flashlight and find the three stars making up Orion's Belt. From the belt, locate the other stars in this constellation. Note that the constellation at the bottom of the map will be found nearer the horizon you are facing.
4. Using the procedure in step 3, find the other constellations on the map. Check your map as often as necessary to find the different star patterns. Note that some of the constellations are toward the east and some are overhead. If necessary, reposition your chair so that you can best view the constellations by simply turning your head.
5. Locate these seven stars: Capella, Castor, Pollux, Procyon, Sirius, Rigel, and Aldebaran. Imagine a curved line connecting the stars in order, then continue the line to connect Aldebaran to Capella.

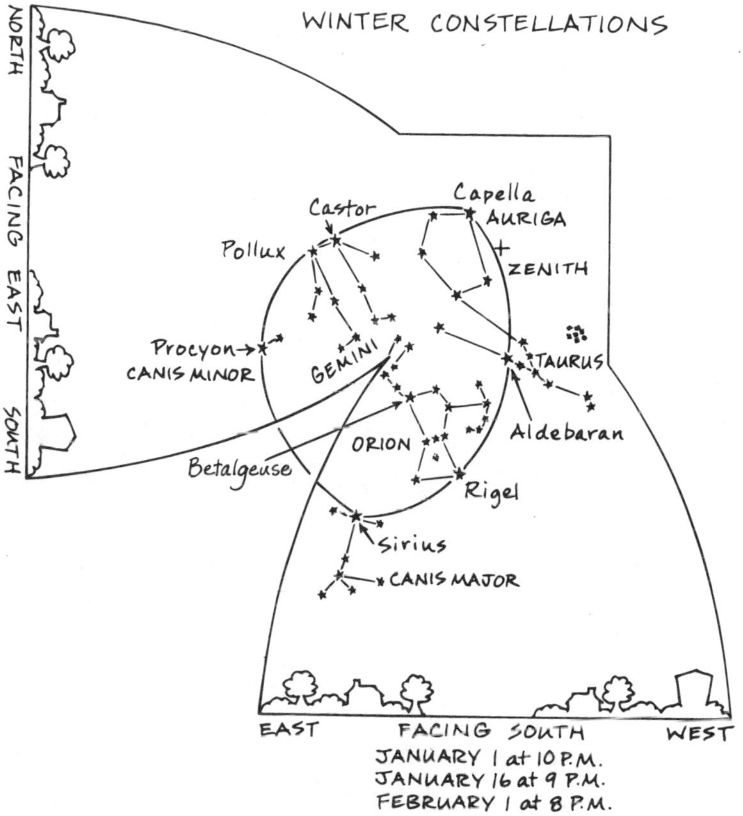

Results

When the seven stars are connected with a curved imaginary line, a circle is formed.

Why?

The circle connecting the seven stars is called the Winter Circle. There is no specific order necessary in locating the stars, but it's usually easy to find Orion's Belt, so that's a good place to start.

BOOK LIST

Mayo, Gretchen Will. *More Star Tales.* New York: Walker, 1991. A collection of Indian legends about stars and other celestial bodies in the nighttime sky.

Raymo, Chet. *365 Starry Nights.* New York: Simon & Schuster, 1982. A description and star map for each night of the year.

VanCleave, Janice. *Constellations for Every Kid.* New York: Wiley, 1997. Fun, simple constellation experiments, including information about Orion and many other seasonal constellations.

MORE FUN WITH STARS!

Stars vary in color. Astronomers use an instrument called a **spectroscope** to separate starlight into light rays, which are seen as a band of colors called a **spectrum.** The spectrum of a star gives astronomers information about the star, such as its temperature. Use a compact disc (CD) to show how light can be separated into a spectrum. Hold the CD so that sunlight coming through a window or light from a lamp hits its shiny side. *CAUTION: Never look directly at the Sun, and don't reflect the light to your eyes because doing so can damage them.* Move the CD back and forth several times. Observe the color patterns on the CD.

16

Winter Solstice

DID YOU KNOW?

At the North Pole, the stars can sometimes be seen 24 hours a day!

At Earth's equator, there is an equal amount of daylight and darkness each day of the year, but the amount of light in other areas of Earth changes from season to season. Because Earth is tilted on its axis in relation to the Sun, the farther north or south you go from the equator, the more variation there is between the hours of darkness and daylight. The winter solstice occurs on or about December 22 in the **Northern Hemisphere** (region of Earth north of the equator). On this day, the North Pole is tilted so far away from the Sun that the sky is dark there all day and night. This means that stars can be seen 24 hours a day at the North Pole. This date is also the first day of summer in the **Southern Hemisphere** (region of Earth south of the equator). At the South Pole on December 22, it never gets dark!

FUN TIME!

Purpose

To model the light and dark areas of Earth during the winter solstice.

Materials

marker
2-inch (5-cm) -diameter Styrofoam ball
6-inch (15-cm) -square piece of aluminum foil

Procedure

1. Use the marker to make two dots opposite each other on the Styrofoam ball. Label the dots N and S to represent the North and South Poles.
2. Draw a circle around the middle of the ball between the poles to represent the equator. Then draw a circle around each pole, making the two circles the same size. The circle around the North Pole represents the Arctic Circle, and the one around the **South Pole** (the south end of Earth's axis) the Antarctic Circle.
3. Mold the aluminum foil around the ball so that it covers half of the ball from pole to pole. Keep the foil loose enough that the ball moves freely. The foil cup represents the half of Earth that is lighted by the Sun.

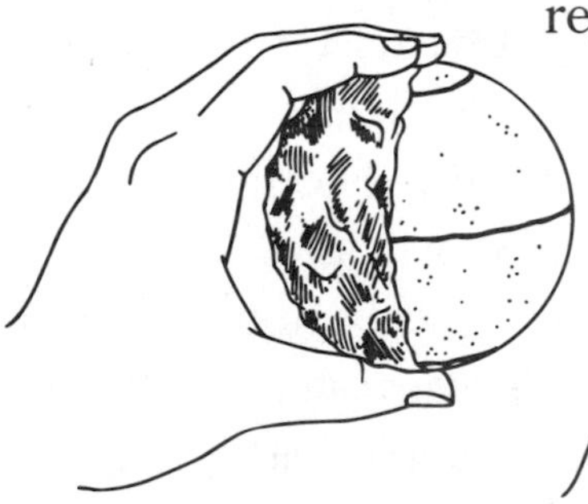

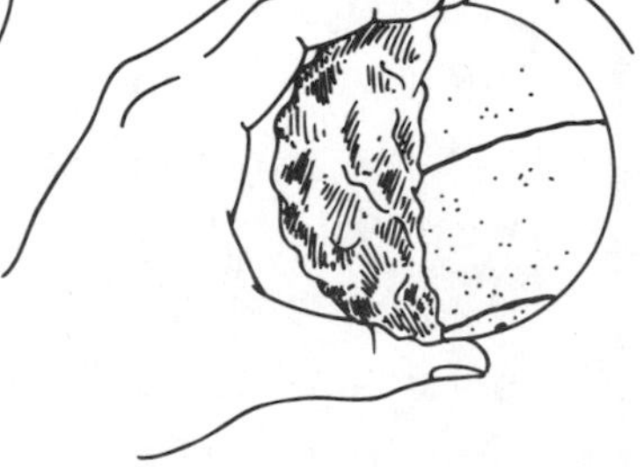

4. Holding the foil stationary, tilt the ball so that the North Pole moves under the foil until the Arctic Circle is just under the edge of the foil. Note that the Antarctic Circle is now completely outside the foil.

Results

The part of the Earth model that is facing the Sun (covered in foil) changes when you tilt the ball, until all of the circle around the North Pole is covered by the foil and none of the circle around the South Pole is covered.

Why?

The half of the ball that is covered by foil represents the side of Earth that is facing the Sun. Earth's axis is tilted in relation to the Sun. So as Earth **orbits** (moves in a curved path around) the Sun during the course of the year, the North Pole tilts away from the Sun during part of the year. At the point in Earth's orbit where the North Pole is tilted farthest from the Sun—around December 22, the winter solstice—Earth's Northern Hemisphere has longer hours of darkness and the **Arctic region** (area north of the **Arctic Circle,** which is latitude 66.5°N) is in complete darkness all 24 hours of that day. As Earth continues in its orbit, the North Pole becomes angled more and more toward the Sun, so more and more of the Northern Hemisphere is lighted. Finally, on June 21, the **summer solstice,** the opposite point in Earth's orbit to the winter solstice, all of the Arctic region is lighted the entire day. The reverse is true for the **Antarctic region** (area south of the **Antarctic Circle,** which is latitude 66.5°S). On December 22, the Antarctic region is lighted and on June 21 it is in darkness.

BOOK LIST

Allison, Linda. *The Reason for Seasons.* Boston: Little, Brown, 1988. Stories to read, ideas to think about, and things to make and do—all contributing to an understanding of the seasons and their effect on Earth.

Rogasky, Barbara. *Winter Poems.* New York: Scholastic Trade, 1994. A collection of winter poems by such authors as Shakespeare, Edgar Allan Poe, and Wallace Stevens.

VanCleave, Janice. *Earth Science for Every Kid.* New York: Wiley, 1991. Fun, simple earth science experiments, including information about the seasons.

MORE FUN WITH LIGHT!

During the winter solstice, the Sun is at its lowest **altitude** (angular height above the horizon—where the sky appears to touch the Earth). The lower the altitude of the Sun, the longer the shadows it produces. How much difference is there between the altitude of the Sun during the winter solstice and its altitude during the summer solstice? You can check by measuring the length of your shadow. At noon on December 22, ask a helper to sketch your shadow on a sidewalk using sidewalk chalk. Measure and record the length of your shadow on this date. Then draw and measure your noontime shadow on June 21 (summer solstice). Compare the length of your summer solstice shadow to that of your winter solstice shadow.

17

Bear's Paws

DID YOU KNOW?

The hair on the bottom of a polar bear's paws helps to keep it from slipping on the ice!

Stopping and starting, walking and running all depend on friction. You slip and slide on ice because there is little friction between the smooth bottom of your shoes and the slippery surface. Polar bears would do the same thing, except for the hair and rough pads on the bottom of their feet, which increase the friction between the paw and the ice. A polar bear paw is about 24 inches (30 cm) wide and 18 inches (45 cm) long and weighs about 25 pounds (11.4 kg)!

FUN TIME!

Purpose

To demonstrate how friction affects sliding on a slick surface.

Materials

- hand towel
- 4 to 6 thick books
- large metal cookie sheet
- small, short, unopened can of food, such as tuna
- wide rubber band

Procedure

1. Lay the towel on a table.
2. Stack the books at one end of the towel.
3. Place one end of the cookie sheet on the towel and the other on the stack of books to make a ramp.
4. Place the can at the top of the ramp and release it. (Be sure to set the can on its bottom, not its side.) Observe the speed at which the can slides down the cookie sheet.
5. Wrap the rubber band around the can from top to bottom.
6. Repeat step 4.

Results

Without the rubber band, the can slides very quickly down the ramp. After the rubber band has been added, the can moves slowly or not at all.

Why?

The rubber band, like the hair and rough pads on a bear's paw, increases the friction between it and the slick surface of the cookie sheet. As friction increases, the ability of an object to move decreases.

BOOK LIST

Bailey, Jill. *Polar Bear Rescue: Earth's Endangered Creature.* Austin, TX: Steck-Vaughn Library, 1991. A biologist, a television broadcaster, and an Iñuit family observe the habits and habitat of the polar bear.

VanCleave, Janice. *Physics for Every Kid.* New York: Wiley, 1991. Fun, simple physics experiments, including information about friction.

MORE FUN WITH POLAR BEARS!

The average male polar bear weighs about 1,000 pounds (454 kg), and a female about half this much. Their weight doesn't keep them from being very active and athletic as they jump around on the ice. In fact, their weight increases the pressure of their bodies on the ice, which can help to prevent their sliding. You can demonstrate this by getting down on your hands and knees on a smooth floor. Lightly push one hand against the floor and slide it forward. Notice how easily your hand slides across the floor if light pressure is applied. Repeat, pressing your hand more firmly against the floor. Notice the change as a result of increased pressure.

18

Cool Sunglasses

DID YOU KNOW?

Ancient sunglasses were made of bone!

Early Eskimos, including the Iñupiat and the Iñuit, natives of the Arctic region, are known to have used a kind of sunglasses to protect their eyes from sunlight. In their environment, sunlight reflecting off snow, ice, and water could be blindingly bright. The Iñuit made early versions of sunglasses from natural materials, such as antlers, wood, and bone. They carved these materials into coverings for their eyes, with slits that allowed only a small portion of light in.

Modern sunglasses with colored lenses work by filtering the light so that only some of the light reaches your eyes. White light is visible light that is made up of all the rainbow colors of light. If white light passes through clear lenses, all of the colors pass through together. But when white light passes through colored lenses, some colors of light are blocked by the lenses and some pass through. The darker the lens, the fewer colors of light it allows to pass through.

FUN TIME!

Purpose

To discover how a small opening can decrease the light you see.

Materials

scissors
2-inch (5-cm) -square piece of black construction paper
sharpened pencil
desk lamp
adult helper

Procedure

1. Cut a circle with about a 2-inch (5-cm) diameter from the paper.
2. Ask an adult to use the point of the pencil to make a tiny hole in the center of the paper.
3. With the light off, turn the lamp so that it faces you.
4. With your face at least 2 feet (60 cm) from the bulb, hold the black circle over one eye and close your other eye.
5. Ask your helper to turn on the lamp. Look at the bulb through the tiny hole in the paper and note how bright the light is. Remove the paper and look at the light. Again note how bright the light is.

Results

The light looks less bright when it is viewed through the small hole.

Why?

When you look at the light through the small hole, most of it is blocked by the paper. Only a small amount of light passes through the hole into your eye. This is similar to the way that the Iñuit sunglasses worked.

BOOK LIST

Ardley, Neil. *The Science Book of Light.* New York: Harcourt Brace, 1991. Simple experiments demonstrate basic principles of light.

Shemie, Bonnie. *Houses of Snow, Skin, and Bones.* Tundra Books, 1989. The materials and methods used by the Iñuit to build shelter in a freezing environment.

Taylor, Barbara. *Arctic and Antarctic.* New York: Knopf, 1995. A description of Earth's frozen poles and the human and animal life that survive at subzero temperatures, including a 4,000-year-old Iñuit tribe in the Arctic and the king penguins of the Antarctic, who dive deep into frigid seas filled with icebergs the size of Massachusetts.

VanCleave, Janice. *Physics for Every Kid.* New York: Wiley, 1991. Fun, simple physics experiments, including information about light.

MORE FUN WITH SUNGLASSES!

Design and make sunglasses similar to those made by the Iñuit. Instead of bone and wood, use materials such as poster board and string. Draw glasses on a piece of poster board, then cut them out. Cut out small horizontal eye slits. Use a paper punch to make holes in each end of your glasses. Tie a string through each hole. Decorate your glasses with crayons or markers, then put the glasses on and tie the strings behind your head.

Winter

19

Sweet Crystals

DID YOU KNOW?

Sugar is a natural antifreeze!

The temperature of the water in the Antarctic and Arctic Oceans is just below freezing for most of the year. The waters of McMurdo Sound in the Ross Sea off Antarctica are among the coldest in the world. The surface of this water is likely to be covered with ice for 10 months of the year. Fish, such as the dragonfish, swim in the frigid salt water below the ice. While salt in the water helps to keep this water from freezing, a special sugar-like substance in the blood of the fish, called **glycopeptide,** helps to keep ice from forming inside the fish. Like antifreeze, which when added to the water in a car's radiator keeps the water from turning to ice, glycopeptide keeps the blood of these fish from freezing. This natural antifreeze sticks to any tiny ice crystals in the blood and prevents them from growing large enough to be damaging.

FUN TIME!

Purpose

To show how sugar affects the formation of ice crystals.

Materials

- two 5-ounce (150-ml) paper cups
- tap water
- masking tape
- marking pen
- 1 tablespoon (15 ml) sugar
- spoon
- freezer

Procedure

1. Fill both cups about half full with water.
2. Use the tape and pen to label one of the cups S, for sugar.
3. Add the sugar to the water in the labeled cup and stir.
4. Set both cups in the freezer.
5. Allow the cups to sit in the freezer overnight.
6. Squeeze the cups to determine how firm their contents are.

Results

The sugar-water ice feels mushy, but the ice made from water without sugar is hard.

Why?

The water molecules in each cup combine to form ice crystals. In the water without sugar, the crystals grow as more water molecules are added to them. In time, all the crystals combine, forming one solid block of ice. In the sugar water, the sugar molecules prevent the ice crystals from combining, so only small ice crystals form.

BOOK LIST

Markle, Sandra. *Pioneering Frozen Worlds.* New York: Atheneum Books for Young Readers, 1996. An exciting introduction to Earth's frozen polar regions. Describes glaciers, icebergs, sea ice, and animals, including dragonfish.

Penny, Malcolm. *Polar Seas.* Austin, TX: Raintree/Steck-Vaughn, 1997. Describes the geography, plants, animals, trade, and resources of the polar seas.

VanCleave, Janice. *Chemistry for Every Kid.* New York: Wiley, 1989. Fun, simple chemistry experiments, including information about the effect of sugar on ice crystals.

MORE FUN WITH ICE!

Any substance dissolved in water causes ice crystals to be smaller. These smaller ice crystals make the ice softer. Ice pops are an example of soft ice. Here's how to make your own ice pops. Pour 1 quart (1 liter) of water into a pitcher and add 1 package, 0.15 ounces (4.3 g), of unsweetened flavored powdered drink mix and 1½ cups (375 ml) of granulated sugar. Stir. Fill twelve 3-ounce (90-ml) paper cups with the drink. Cover each cup with a piece of aluminum foil. Push a craft stick through the foil covering of each cup and stand the stick vertically in the cup. Set the cups in the freezer. (You may want to put them all on a plate to keep them from getting knocked over.) The next day, remove a cup from the freezer, take the foil and paper cup off, and enjoy your ice pop.

20

Snowflakes

DID YOU KNOW?

An 8-inch (20-cm) snowflake once fell in Siberia!

Snow is composed of small crystals of frozen water called **snow crystals.** These crystals begin to form when water **vapor** (gas) in the air **condenses** (changes from a vapor to a liquid) on a dust particle to make a tiny water drop. The water drop is lifted high in the **atmosphere** (blanket of air around Earth) where the temperature is below freezing, and the drop freezes into a tiny ice crystal. If the temperature is around 5°F (-15°C) and there is plenty of water vapor, the ice crystal grows six branches with arms and is called a snow crystal. Snow crystals grow as water vapor freezes on them. The process by which a vapor changes directly to a solid or a solid to a gas without becoming a liquid is called **sublimation.** The shapes of the crystals vary, but all are basically **hexagonal** (six-sided). The exact shape depends mainly on temperature.

As snow crystals fall through the clouds, they collide with other snow crystals, forming **snowflakes.** The size of the snowflake depends on the number of crystals in it. As the moisture content of the air increases, more snow crystals form, thus more of them will collide to form larger flakes. A 2-inch (5-cm) snowflake is considered very large, so the 8-inch (20-cm) snowflake measured in Bratsk, Siberia, in 1971 was a mega-snowflake.

As snowflakes fall to the ground, air is trapped between them. So newly fallen **snow** (snowflakes that fall and collect on the ground) is light and fluffy because of the great amount of air mixed with it.

FUN TIME!

Purpose

To show that snow contains trapped air.

Materials

10-ounce (300-ml) transparent plastic glass
snow (or shaved or finely crushed ice if snow is not available)
ruler

Procedure

1. Scrape the glass across the snow to fill it. Take care not to pack the snow in the glass. Fresh snow works best.
2. Scrape the edge of the ruler across the top of the glass to remove snow above the glass. This levels the snow across the top of the glass.
3. Allow the glass to sit at room temperature until the snow melts.
4. Note the amount of water in the glass.

Results

When the glass of snow has melted, the water produced does not fill the glass.

The volume of snow is greater than the volume of liquid water it becomes when melted. Shaved or crushed ice is a mixture of small ice crystals and air. Like snow, ice has a greater volume than the water it becomes when melted.

Why?

The more air that is mixed with the snow, the greater the volume of the snow. When the snow melts, the air in the mixture is released.

BOOK LIST

Archer, Cheryl. *Snow Watch.* Buffalo, NY: Kids Can Press, 1997. Fun indoor and outdoor activities about snow, as well as information about snowflake formation, glacier movement, the world's largest ice cube (Antarctica), the true color of snow, how to catch a snowflake and keep it, and much, much more!

Bianchi, John. *Snow: Learning for the Fun of It.* Tundra Books, 1992. A wealth of information about snow and how it affects people.

Kohl, MaryAnn and Jean Potter. *Science Arts.* Bellingham, WA: Bright Ring, 1993. A book of science discovery art projects including snow investigations.

VanCleave, Janice. *Weather.* New York: Wiley, 1995. Experiments about snow and other weather topics. Each chapter contains ideas that can be turned into award-winning science fair projects.

MORE FUN WITH SNOWFLAKES!

Make paper models of snowflakes by folding a round basket-type coffee filter in half. Fold the half in thirds, then fold that piece in half. Cut across the pointed tip and cut a large notch in the folded corner. Make cuts anywhere on the sides of the remaining piece. Unfold the paper and you have a hexagonal snowflake.

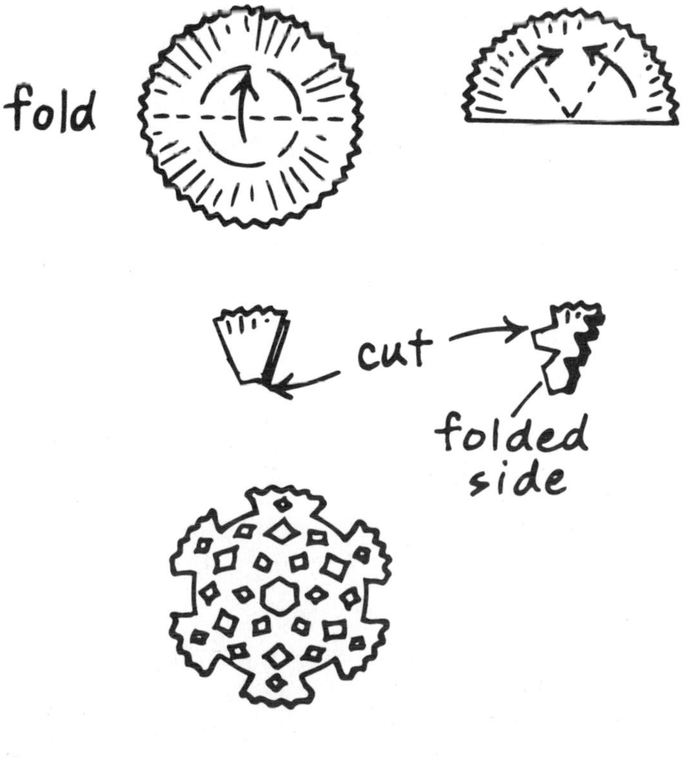

21

Snow Motion

DID YOU KNOW?

Snowflakes sometimes go up!

Like everything on or near Earth, gravity pulls snowflakes toward the ground. As snowflakes move through the air, friction between the snowflakes and the air around them causes the flakes to fall very slowly. The larger and flatter the shape of the snowflake, the greater the friction between it and the air. As with a parachute, a strong updraft of air can lift snowflakes, until gravity again takes over and pulls them down.

FUN TIME!

Purpose

To demonstrate the difference in rate of fall between a snowflake and a raindrop.

Materials

two 9-inch (22.5-cm) round balloons

Procedure

1. Inflate one of the balloons and tie it.
2. Holding the balloons, one in each hand, raise the balloons about chest high, then release them at the same time.
3. Observe the falling balloons to determine which one falls faster.

Results

The inflated balloon falls more slowly than the uninflated balloon.

Why?

The weight of the two balloons is about the same. (The air inside the inflated balloon increases the weight of the inflated balloon only slightly.) But the inflated balloon has a larger volume, which gives it a larger surface area. As the balloons fall, the increased surface area of the inflated balloon increases the friction between it and the air it falls through. So the inflated balloon falls more slowly. The inflated balloon represents a snowflake and the uninflated balloon a raindrop, each with the same number of water molecules and about the same weight, but different surface areas.

BOOK LIST

Caney, Steven. *Kids' America.* New York: Workman Publishing, 1978. Activities, projects, and legends about America, including how to make a snow globe with around-the-house materials.

Otfinoski, Steven. *Blizzards.* Twenty-First Century Books, 1995. Eyewitness accounts and photos of the devastating impact of blizzards.

VanCleave, Janice. *Earth Science for Every Kid.* New York: Wiley, 1991. Fun, simple earth science experiments, including information about snowflakes.

———. *Weather.* New York: Wiley, 1995. Experiments about snowflakes and other weather topics. Each chapter contains ideas that can be turned into award-winning science fair projects.

MORE FUN WITH SNOWFLAKES!

As air hits against snowflakes, they are moved about in different directions. This is why they flutter around as they fall. Demonstrate the movement of snowflakes hit by moving air particles by throwing the inflated balloon into the air, then tapping the bottom of the balloon with the eraser end of a pencil. Make a game out of it. Challenge a friend to keep the balloon suspended in the air longer than you can.

22

Moon Rings

DID YOU KNOW?

You can sometimes see "rainbows" at night!

Sometimes at night you can see a rainbow of colors around the Moon. This crown of colors, called a **lunar corona,** is not exactly like the rainbow we see during the daytime, but it is caused by the same thing—rays of light being **diffracted** (bent around an object) by water drops suspended in Earth's atmosphere. Diffraction separates the light around the Moon into colors, starting from the edge of the Moon. While all the colors of the rainbow can be seen, red and blue are usually more prominent.

The size of the water drops suspended in Earth's atmosphere affects the colors and size of the corona. Small water droplets produce the largest corona, and those of uniform size produce the brightest colors. Clouds with a variety of droplet sizes produce a deformed corona with blurred colors. A bright full moon shining through a thin layer of small uniform droplets, such as in **altostratus clouds** (flat, layered clouds at high altitudes), produces the most beautiful corona.

FUN TIME!

Purpose

To demonstrate a lunar corona.

Materials

freezer
10-ounce (300-ml) clear plastic glass
desk lamp

Procedure

1. Place the glass in the freezer for 5 minutes or more.
2. Turn on the lamp in an otherwise darkened room.
3. Position the lamp so the bulb is visible.
4. Take the glass out of the freezer and exhale on its cold surface.
5. Stand across the room and look through the glass at the lightbulb.

Results

You see a rainbow of colors around the lightbulb.

Why?

The water vapor from your breath condenses on the cold glass to form a layer of tiny water droplets. When you look at the light through the tiny droplets, the droplets diffract the light and separate it into colors, just as water droplets in a cloud in Earth's atmosphere diffract the light around the Moon, creating a lunar corona.

BOOK LIST

Bredeson, Carmen. *The Moon.* Danbury, CT: Franklin Watts, 1998. Describes what people have believed about the Moon and what has been learned over time. Also presents an overview of the Apollo space program.

Lynch, David K. *Color and Light in Nature.* New York: Cambridge University Press, 1995. Clear explanations of over 100 naturally occurring optical phenomena visible to the naked eye, including shadows, mirages, and halos.

Rau, Dana Meachen. *One Giant Step.* Norwalk, CT: Soundprints Corp. Audio, 1996. While on a field trip to the National Air and Space Museum, Tommy imagines himself as Neil Armstrong, who was the Mission Commander aboard *Apollo 11* and the first man to set foot on the Moon.

VanCleave, Janice. *Astronomy for Every Kid.* New York: Wiley, 1991. Fun, simple astronomy experiments, including information about the Moon.

———. *Solar System.* New York: Wiley, 2000. Experiments about the Moon and other solar system topics. Each chapter contains ideas that can be turned into award-winning science fair projects.

MORE FUN WITH MOONLIGHT!

Halos can also be seen around the Moon. A **halo** is a white or faintly colored ring around the Moon. Unlike a corona, a halo doesn't appear to touch the Moon, nor break its light into rainbow colors. Halos form when moonlight reflects off ice crystals in Earth's atmosphere. These crystals may be free-falling or they may occur within thin layers of **cirrus clouds** (white, wispy clouds made of ice crystals that occur at high altitudes). Winter is a good time to look for lunar halos, but they may occur at other times of the year. They are more common in high latitudes, such as nearer the Arctic or Antarctic Circles. According to weather folklore, lunar coronas mean good weather is coming, while lunar halos predict bad weather. Observe the Moon as often as possible, checking for the presence of a corona or halo. When you see one, note the weather conditions that follow. Is there any truth to the folklore?

23

Heartbeat

DID YOU KNOW?

Your heart beats about 135,000 times each day!

Your heart is a hollow, muscular **organ** (part of a living thing that performs a special job) that pumps blood through **blood vessels** (tubes through which blood flows) throughout your body. Every time your heart pumps, blood is pushed out away from the heart through blood vessels called **arteries.** These arteries stretch and bulge. This stretching with each heartbeat is your **pulse.** Your heart beats day in and day out without your thinking about it. Physical exercise, or being anxious about your special valentine, makes your heart work harder and squeeze even more frequently.

FUN TIME!

Purpose

To demonstrate how hard your heart works.

Materials

timer
tennis ball
pencil
paper
helper

Procedure

1. Ask your helper to be the timekeeper. When your helper says start, squeeze the ball as many times as possible, counting each squeeze.
2. When your helper says stop, at the end of 15 seconds, record the number of squeezes. Note how your hand feels.
3. Multiply the number of squeezes by 4 to determine the number of squeezes that would be made if you kept squeezing at the same pace for 60 seconds, or 1 minute. For example, if you made 40 squeezes in 15 seconds, then:

   $40 \times 4 = 160$ squeezes in 60 seconds (1 minute)

Results

You probably will have squeezed the ball about 40 times in 15 seconds. Even after just 15 seconds of squeezing, your hand muscles feel tired.

Why?

Each time your heart beats, it squeezes about as hard as you squeezed the tennis ball with your hand. At rest, an adult's heart beats about 70 times a minute and a child's about 95 times a minute.

BOOK LIST

Brownrigg, Sheri. *Hearts and Craft.* Berkeley, CA: Tricycle Press, 1995. Valentine crafts with quotes from writers, including Louisa May Alcott.

Hurst, J. Willis. *The Heart: The Kids' Question and Answer Book.* New York: McGraw-Hill, 1998. A doctor answers kids' questions about the heart in an easily understandable way.

Suzane, Jamie. *Big Brother's in Love Again.* New York: Bantam Skylark, 1997. Steven has to make a choice as to who his true valentine is.

VanCleave, Janice. *Human Body for Every Kid.* New York: Wiley, 1995. Fun, simple human body experiments, including information about the heart.

MORE FUN WITH HEARTS!

The earliest Valentine's Day card still in existence is in the British Museum. The card was sent in 1415 by Charles, duke of Orleans, to his wife while he was imprisoned in the Tower of London. Possibly there was a hidden meaning in the duke's message. You can make a special valentine with a secret message. Copy the envelope pattern shown here. Cut around the outside of the envelope, then cut out the heart-shaped piece. Fold the bottom section of the envelope and the two tabs along the fold lines. Use small pieces of tape to secure the tabs as shown so you have a small envelope.

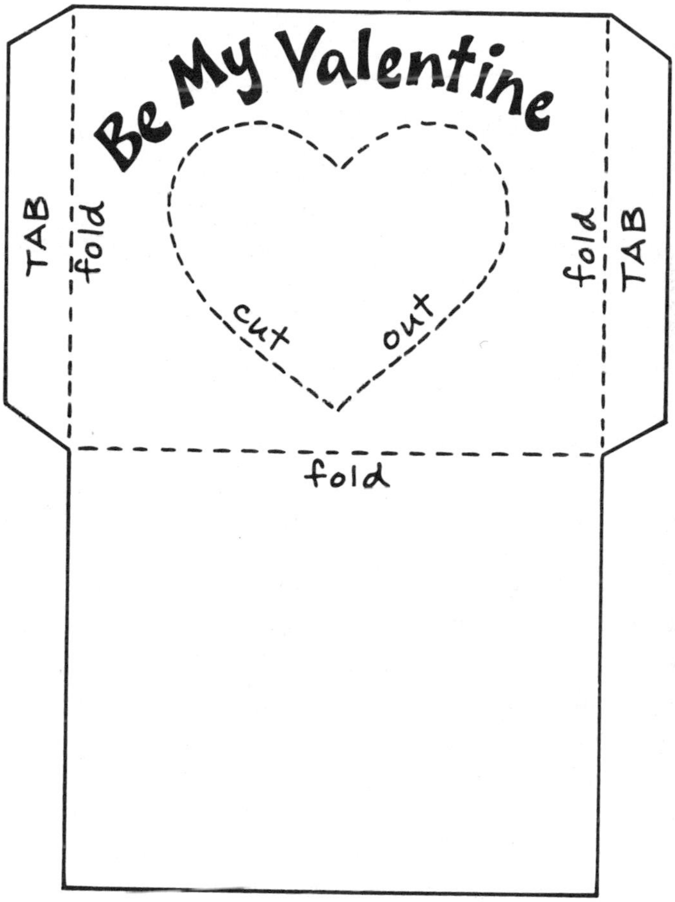

Turn the envelope so that the heart-shaped cutout is faceup. With a yellow felt-tip pen, print a secret message, such as the one shown, inside the heart. Cut out a square of plastic from a red, transparent, plastic report folder to fit in the envelope. Insert the red plastic square in the envelope. Note that your secret message disappears behind the red plastic. Tell the recipient of the valentine to remove the red plastic to read your secret message.

Winter

24

Fat Facts

DID YOU KNOW?

Animals store fat for the winter!

Fat not only insulates the body of an animal but is also needed as stored energy and cushions the body from injuries. Fat is an essential nutrient that comes from the foods that an animal eats. It is also produced by the animal's body and stored for future use. Animals often store fat for the winter, when there is less food available.

When needed, stored fat is changed so that it can be used by the animal's body to make energy. In **vertebrates** (animals with backbones), this change is made by juices in an organ called the **liver.** One of the jobs of an animal's liver is to produce **bile,** a juice that helps digest fat by physically breaking it into tiny globules just as dishwashing liquid breaks up grease on dishes. These fat globules can then be chemically digested, which means they are chemically changed into simpler substances that can be used by the animal's body cells.

FUN TIME!

Purpose

To demonstrate how fat is broken into small globules.

Materials

pen
2 index cards
2 small cereal bowls
tap water
measuring spoon
2 teaspoons (10 ml) cooking oil
desk lamp
spoon
timer
1 teaspoon (5 ml) dishwashing liquid

Procedure

1. Use the pen to label the cards A and B.
2. Fill the bowls half full with water.
3. Add 1 teaspoon (5 ml) of cooking oil to each bowl.
4. Set the bowls under the desk lamp, one on each card. Observe the contents of the bowls.
5. Vigorously stir bowl A with the spoon.

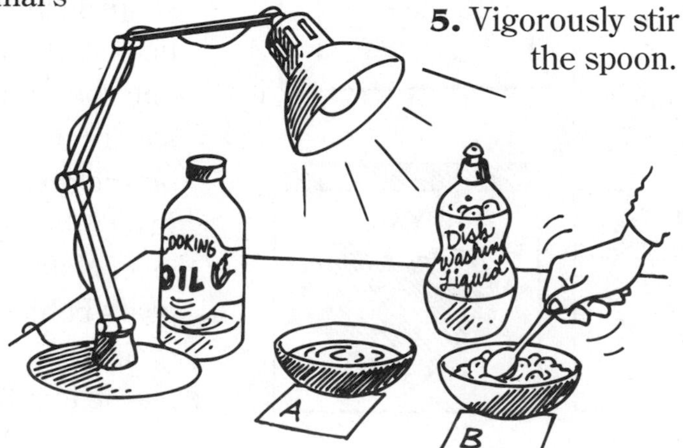

6. Observe the bowl's contents immediately, then again after 5 minutes.
7. Add the dishwashing liquid to bowl B.
8. Repeat steps 5 and 6 with bowl B.

Results

Before stirring, the **oil** (liquid fat) generally formed a thin layer on the surface of the water in each bowl. After stirring, the oil in bowl A broke into small globules and mixed with the water. But after standing, the oil separated from the water and formed pads of oil that floated on the water's surface and in time formed one layer. In bowl B, stirring produced a foam and the oil broke into tiny globules that mixed with the water. After standing, some of the tiny globules remained mixed with the water.

Why?

Stirring a mixture of two liquids that do not dissolve in each other, such as oil and water, causes one of the liquids (oil) to be suspended in little drops in the other liquid (water). This result is called an **emulsion.** If allowed to stand, the liquids in an emulsion separate, as did the oil and water in bowl A. If an **emulsifier** (substance that prevents an emulsion from separating) such as dishwashing liquid is used, the emulsion does not separate, as in bowl B. In an animal's body, bile does the same job on fats that the dishwashing liquid did on the oil in this experiment. Bile physically digests fat by breaking it into small globules so they can be chemically digested.

BOOK LIST

Ontario Science Center. *Foodworks.* Perseus Press, 1987. Over 100 science activities and fascinating facts that explore the magic of food.

Silverstein, Alvin. *Fats (Food Power!).* Brookfield, CT: Millbrook Press, 1992. Describes fats and their function in your diet.

VanCleave, Janice. *Nutrition for Every Kid.* New York: Wiley, 1999. Fun, simple nutrition experiments, including information about fat.

MORE FUN WITH FAT!

Oils are liquid at room temperature. Oil and water do not mix. Use this fact to create an interesting painting. Pour 1 teaspoon (5 ml) of cooking oil into a saucer. Dip a cotton swab in the oil and use the wet cotton swab to draw a picture in oil on a sheet of white typing paper. Allow the painting to stand for 2 to 3 minutes to allow the oil to thoroughly soak into the paper. Then paint the entire paper, including oily places, with tempera paint in your choice of colors. Allow the paint to dry. Notice the color of the paper where the oil was applied.

25

Penguin Undercoat

DID YOU KNOW?

Penguins have a fatty undercoat that keeps them warm!

The outer fur and feathers of animals helps to **insulate** (reduce the movement of heat energy into or out of) their bodies from the cold. While penguins have feathers, those that live in the Antarctic need additional insulation from their frigid environment. This extra protection is provided by a thick layer of **blubber** (fat) under their skin.

Heat moves from a warmer place to a colder place. **Insulators** (materials that insulate), such as blubber, restrict the movement of heat away from the warm inner body of the penguin to the freezing air or icy ground outside its body. While some heat is lost by the penguin, its body produces more. As long as the loss is not greater than the gain, the penguin stays warm.

FUN TIME!

Purpose

To determine how blubber insulates.

Materials

1 tablespoon (15 ml) shortening
2 plastic sandwich bags
2 ice cubes
timer
helper

Procedure

1. Place the shortening in the palm of one of your hands.
2. Place your hands inside the plastic bags, one in each bag.
3. Cup your hands and ask your helper to place an ice cube on top of each plastic bag.
4. Hold the ice in your hands for about 5 seconds. Compare how cold each hand feels.

Results

The hand without the shortening feels colder.

Why?

The plastic bag represents the skin on an animal, the shortening represents the layer of blubber beneath the skin, and your hand represents the animal's inner body. Your hand feels cold when heat is removed from your body by the ice cube. The shortening insulated your hand from the cold ice cube, so the hand with shortening on it lost less heat and felt warmer.

BOOK LIST

Atwater, Richard. *Mr. Popper's Penguins.* Boston: Little, Brown, 1988. Mr. Popper is a housepainter, but in his imagination he is an Antarctic explorer. The unexpected delivery of a large crate containing an Antarctic penguin changes the life and fortunes of Mr. Popper.

Potter, Keith R. *Seven Weeks on an Iceberg.* San Francisco: Chronicle Books, 1999. This fact-filled book provides information about Antarctica and the animals that live there, including how penguins keep warm, why they are black and white, and why they don't live somewhere warmer.

VanCleave, Janice. *Animals.* New York: Wiley, 1993. Experiments about penguins and other animals. Each chapter contains ideas that can be turned into award-winning science fair projects.

MORE FUN WITH PENGUINS!

The male emperor penguin cares for the egg laid by the female by holding it on his feet tucked under the warm skin flap of his belly. The egg stays on its father's feet for about 2 months during the cold, windy, dark Antarctic winter. During this egg-tending time, the male **fasts** (doesn't eat) while the female swims in the frigid ocean, getting fat on gourmet meals of **krill** (small shrimp-like animals). You can get a feel for how difficult it is for the male penguin to walk with an egg on his feet. Pour ½ cup (125 ml) of uncooked rice into a sock. Tie a knot in the sock. This is your "egg." Standing with your feet together, ask a helper to place the sock on top of your feet. Try to walk without dropping the sock off your feet. Note that your "egg" stays on your feet a bit more easily than the penguin's egg because it does not easily roll around. But the penguin has a flap of skin that folds over his egg to help hold it in place.

Winter

26

Turtle Warm-ups

DID YOU KNOW?

Some turtles spend the winter underground!

Most turtles live in areas with warm climates but some live in regions with cold winters. Turtles are cold-blooded, which means their body temperature changes with the temperature of their environment. When a turtle's body temperature drops, the turtle finds a sunny spot. The energy from the Sun heats its body and raises its body temperature.

If the outdoor temperature is too low, a turtle's body cools faster than the Sun can warm it, so it must find a protective place to stay. Turtles can survive periods of low temperature by seeking a place, such as underground, where the temperature will not fall below freezing, except temporarily. A turtle hibernates, living in a sleep-like state of partial or total inactivity in which its body temperature is lower than usual. In this state the turtle's body activities, such as heart and breathing rates, are slowed down, reducing the need for food, water, and air. The turtle survives off the fat stored in its body, and there is enough air in its underground hole to breathe.

FUN TIME!

Purpose

To demonstrate the difference between the change of land and air temperatures.

Materials

2 outdoor thermometers
two 10-ounce (300-ml) plastic glasses
soil
freezer

Procedure

1. Stand a thermometer in each glass.
2. Fill one of the glasses with 1 inch (2.5 cm) of soil.
3. Leave the other glass alone. It is filled with air.
4. Allow the glasses to stand at room temperature for 1 hour or until the soil and air reach the same temperature.
5. Record the temperature on each thermometer, then place both glasses in the freezer.
6. Every 10 minutes for 30 minutes, record the temperature on each thermometer.

Results

After being in the freezer, the temperature of the soil is higher than the temperature of the air in the cup.

Why?

For a material's temperature to decrease, the material must lose heat. The air in the cup placed in the freezer was warmer than the air in the freezer. Since warm air is less dense than cold air, it rises and cold air sinks. Because of the differences in the density of air at different temperatures, there was a movement of cold air into the cup and warm air out of the cup. Soil in the cup as on Earth loses heat slowly, so the soil stays warm for a long time while the warm air above is being replaced with colder, denser air. So during the winter when the air above the ground is cold, animals can burrow (dig) into the soil and stay warm.

BOOK LIST

Bailed, Jill. *Operation Turtle.* Austin, TX: Raintree/Steck-Vaughn, 1992. Ernie and his aides tag sea turtles as they come onto the beach to lay eggs. Fictional story combined with factual information focuses on the behavior and endangered status of the sea turtle.

Patterson, Jordan. *Box Turtles: Keeping and Breeding Them in Captivity.* Broomall, PA: Chelsea House, 1998. Information about the physical characteristics, behavior, health, and breeding of box turtles and how you can keep them as pets.

VanCleave, Janice. *Animals.* New York: Wiley, 1993. Experiments about animal behavior and other animal topics. Each chapter contains ideas that can be turned into award-winning science fair projects.

MORE FUN WITH TURTLES!

A turtle that lives on land is commonly called a tortoise. It is one of the slowest-moving animals on Earth. It takes a tortoise about 5 hours to walk 1 mile (1.6 km), which is a speed of ⅕ mile (0.32 km) per hour. Here is a way to model a slow-moving tortoise.

Draw a large turtle shape on an 8-inch (20-cm) -square piece of poster board as shown. Use a paper punch to make a hole at the top of the turtle's head. Thread both ends of a 1-yard (1-m) string through the hole, making a loop in the string. Place the turtle and loop on the floor and stand a chair leg in the loop. Keeping the loop taut, position the turtle so that the ends of the string extend only about 6 inches (15 cm) outside the hole. Holding the ends of the string at a slight angle to the hole, pull one end at a time and observe the motion of the turtle.

Spring

In spring, you can fly kites in March winds, stand under an umbrella in April showers, and pick colorful May flowers. Discover the new life in this season as you study how flowers open and search for a lucky four-leaf clover. With a large number of bright stars visible on warm evenings, spring is a great time to observe the stars. Spring brings a reminder of how beautiful Earth is. On Earth Day in April, discover new ways to keep our planet clean now and in the future.

DATES TO MARK ON YOUR CALENDAR

- *March 3, 1847,* is the birth date of Alexander Graham Bell, the American scientist who invented the telephone.
- *March 17* is Saint Patrick's Day, honoring the patron saint of Ireland—wear green.
- *On or about March 21* is the **vernal equinox,** the first day of spring. At the equinox, day and night are of equal length.
- *April 3, 1934,* is the birth date of Jane Goodall, the British animal behaviorist best known for her long-term observations of chimpanzees in the wild.
- *April 15, 1452,* is the birth date of Leonardo da Vinci, an Italian artist and scientist. His scientific manuscripts were written with his left hand in right-to-left mirror-image (upside down) script.
- *April 19 to 25* is a great time to view the Lyrid meteor shower, with April 22 probably being the best night to observe.
- *April 22* is Earth Day, a day set aside to remind us to take better care of Earth.
- *May 1 to 10* is the time to look for the Eta Aquarid meteor shower, with May 6 being the best night to observe.
- *May 9, 1926,* is the date that Admiral Richard E. Byrd flew over the North Pole.
- *May 20, 1932,* is the date that Amelia Earhart arrived in Londonderry, Northern Ireland, becoming the first woman to make a solo transatlantic flight.
- *May 23, 1707,* is the birth date of Carolus Linnaeus, the Swedish biologist who came up with a system of grouping and naming all living organisms.

Spring

27

Wind Catchers

DID YOU KNOW?

The first wind socks were Chinese kites!

Wind is air in horizontal motion. It can blow in any direction. One easy way to figure out which way the wind is blowing is to use a **wind sock** (a tapered cloth tube used to indicate wind direction and intensity). A wind sock is usually made of nylon and resembles a sock with the toe cut off. It has one large end that is held open by a fixed ring, and tapers down to a smaller open end. When the wind blows, the wind sock fills with air and its tapered end points in the direction the wind is moving. The wind sock can also tell you the relative strength of the wind. A light wind will not hold the sock straight out. But if the sock is horizontal, there must be a strong wind.

Modern wind socks are based on an ancient Chinese kite design. Chinese kites were used as early as 500 B.C. Some kites were in the shape of dragons to frighten enemies and some were shaped like our modern wind socks. They were also used to indicate the strength and direction of the wind.

FUN TIME!

Purpose

To make a wind catcher.

Materials

- ruler
- pencil
- sheet of 9-by-11-inch (22.5-by-27.5-cm) construction paper (any color)
- scissors
- transparent tape
- four ½-by-8-inch (1.25-by-20-cm) tissue paper strips
- paper punch
- 12-inch (30-cm) piece of yarn

Procedure

1. Using the ruler and pencil, draw two diagonal lines on the construction paper as shown. Draw each line from one corner to a point 3 inches (7.5 cm) from the nearest corner.
2. Cut along the diagonal lines and discard the two triangular end pieces.
3. Slightly overlap the cut edges and secure with tape. A tapered tube is made.
4. Tape the tissue paper strips around the small open end of the paper tube.
5. Use the paper punch to make a hole on opposite sides of the large open end of the paper tube.
6. Tie the ends of the yarn in the holes.
7. Holding the yarn, run with the wind catcher.

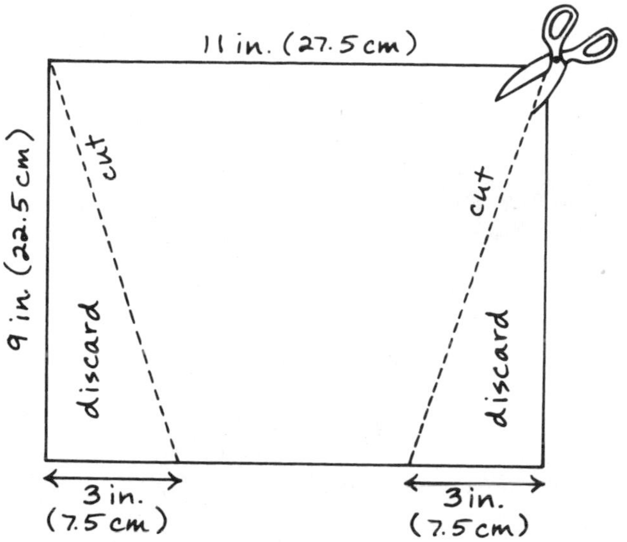

Why?

When you run in one direction, you create a wind that fills the wind catcher and causes it to point in the opposite direction. Because there is a hole in the end of the wind catcher, the wind is allowed to escape. As it moves over the tissue paper streamers, it makes them flutter up and down. When wind fills a hanging wind sock, it causes the small end to point in the direction the wind is blowing.

Results

The wind catcher fills with air and points straight out behind you.

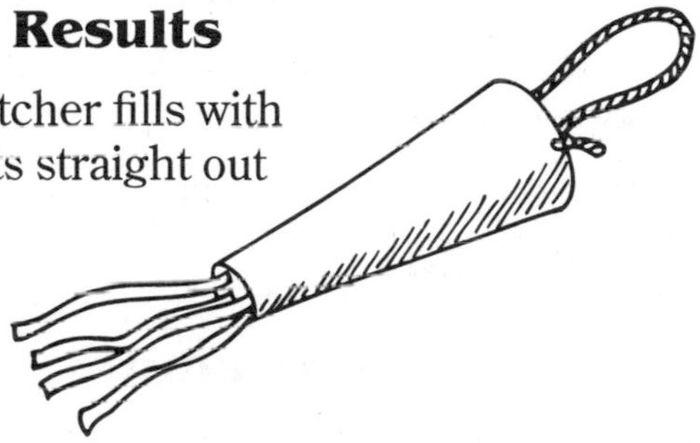

BOOK LIST

Kelly, Emery J. *Kites on the Wind.* Minneapolis, MN: Lerner, 1991. Provides instructions for making 13 kinds of kites that fly without sticks. Includes diagrams and flying tips.

Kennedy, Dorothy M. *Make Things Fly.* New York: Margaret McElderry, 1998. Poems about the wind.

Wolfe, Gretchen. *The Wind at Work.* Chicago: Chicago Review Press, 1997. An introduction to windmills, with activities for understanding some of the principles of wind.

VanCleave, Janice. *Weather.* New York: Wiley, 1995. Experiments about wind and other weather topics. Each chapter contains ideas that can be turned into award-winning science fair projects.

MORE FUN WITH WIND!

Wind chimes are made of objects that make interesting sounds when the wind causes them to bump into each other. Make your own wind chimes by following these steps. Use masking tape to secure a 6-inch (15-cm) piece of string to each of 4 or more metal objects, such as spoons. Tie the free end of the strings to a metal jar ring or small embroidery hoop. The objects should hang so that they can easily bump into one another. Tie a string on opposite sides of the ring to hold the chimes up. Blow on the chimes to test them, and reposition the hanging objects if they do not bump into one another. You may also wish to add more hanging spoons. Hang the wind chimes outdoors, and listen for them the next time the wind blows.

28

Netted

DID YOU KNOW?

Some leaves have fingers!

The blade of a leaf is strengthened by many **veins** (tubes) that run through it. In addition to supporting the leaf, the veins conduct sap. Some of the veins are larger than others, and the arrangement of these larger veins forms two patterns: parallel and netted. In leaves with the **parallel** pattern, such as a lily or grass, the large veins run in the same direction, or nearly so. In leaves with a **netted** pattern, such as a sunflower or an oak tree, the veins branch.

Netted patterns can be grouped into two types: palmate and pinnate. If the large veins in the netted pattern all start at the petiole (stalk) and extend through the blade like fingers on the palm of a hand, the vein pattern is called **palmate.** Leaves of the sugar maple tree are palmate. Leaves divided into separate smaller leaves that radiate from a common point at the petiole, such as clover, horse chestnut, poison ivy, and Virginia creeper, are called **palmate leaflets.** If a single large vein runs through the center of the leaf and smaller veins branch from it like a feather, the pattern is called **pinnate.** Leaves of an oak are pinnate. Leaves divided into separate smaller leaves that are attached along a central petiole, such as the rose, ash, walnut, and hickory, are called **pinnate leaflets.**

FUN TIME!

Purpose

To identify palmate and pinnate leaves.

Materials

park
binoculars
tree and plant field guides (optional)
adult helper

Procedure

1. With your adult helper, take a walk through the park. Use the binoculars and the illustrations shown here to find as many different leaf types as possible.

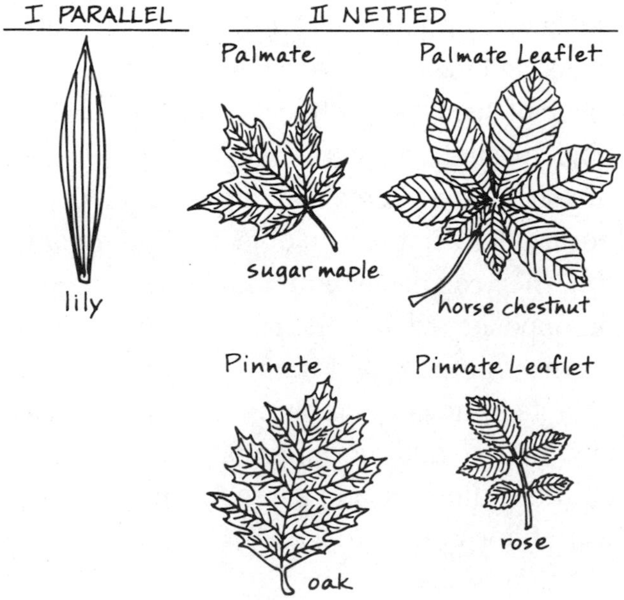

2. Record the number of each type of leaf you find in a table similar to the one shown. Make a mark for each type seen, then add the marks and record a total for each.
3. If you wish, use a field guide to identify specific plants.

Results

Answers will vary depending on the location where leaves are observed.

Why?

The shape of their leaves is one way to tell plants apart.

BOOK LIST

Burner, David. *Trees.* Eyewitness Books. New York: Knopf, 1988. Photographs show different kinds of leaves as well as other information about trees.

Cassie, Brian, and Margorie Burns. *Trees.* National Audubon Society First Field Guide. New York: Scholastic Trade, 1999. A detailed and colorfully illustrated guide to trees of North America.

Niering, William. *Familiar Flowers of North America: Eastern Region.* New York: Knopf, 1987. A field guide to Eastern North American flowers. Photographs include leaves.

———. *Familiar Flowers of North America: Western Region.* New York: Knopf, 1987. A field guide to Western North American flowers. Photographs include leaves.

VanCleave, Janice. *Plants.* New York: Wiley, 1996. Fun, simple plant experiments, including information about leaves. Each chapter contains ideas that can be turned into award-winning science fair projects.

Leaf ID

Leaf Type	Observed	Total
Parallel		
Netted		
Palmate		
Palmate leaflets		
Pinnate		
Pinnate leaflets		

MORE FUN WITH LEAVES!

You can prepare a colorful permanent leaf collection by making leaf rubbings. So that you select safe leaves, ask an adult to assist you in collecting different types of leaves. Make the rubbing by placing 4 to 5 sheets of newspaper on a table. Lay a leaf with its rough, vein side up. Cover the leaf with a sheet of white unlined paper. Rub the side of a crayon back and forth across the paper over the leaf. You will see a colored print of the leaf appear on the paper. Using plant books, identify the plant the leaf came from. Write the name of the plant on the paper. You may wish to add other information, such as the date and where the leaf was found. Repeat the process with each leaf. The rubbings can be placed in a binder.

29

Clover Leaves

DID YOU KNOW?

Finding a four-leaf clover is lucky!

According to Irish folklore, finding a stem of clover (also called a shamrock) with four leaves brings good luck, but finding a clover stem with more than four leaves brings bad luck. Clover usually has stems with three leaves. But sometimes they do grow four, or even more leaves. This is very rare, however, so if you found a four-leaf clover you would be lucky, but it wouldn't bring you luck. This idea is a **superstition** (a belief not based on knowledge). Even so, it is fun to look for four-leaf clovers.

Patrick, patron saint of Ireland, died on March 15 in or about the year 461. It is said that he once used a three-leafed shamrock to explain the Holy Trinity (God the Father, Son, and Holy Spirit). In the years following Saint Patrick's death, in order to honor his memory, people wore shamrocks on March 15. The first public celebration of Saint Patrick's Day in America was 1737. Saint Patrick's Day is now celebrated on March 17.

FUN TIME!

Purpose

To examine clover leaves.

Materials

clover patch

magnifying lens

Procedure

1. Count the leaves on as many clover stems as possible.
2. Record the number of stems you counted and the number that contained four or more leaves.
3. Use the magnifying lens to observe the vein pattern on three or more clover leaves.

Results

You probably didn't find any four-leaf clovers, but you did notice that each stem has three leaves and each leaf has a netted vein pattern. Clover is an example of a palmate leaflet.

Why?

A clover leaf is commonly made up of three leaflets that radiate from a common point at the petiole. This arrangement of leaves is called a palmate leaflet. For more information on palmate leaflets, see chapter 28, "Netted."

BOOK LIST

Barth, Edna. *Shamrocks, Harps, and Shillelaghs.* New York: Houghton Mifflin, 1982. Explores the origin and meaning of the symbols and legends associated with Saint Patrick's Day.

Markham, Marion M. *The St. Patrick's Day Shamrock Mystery.* New York: Houghton Mifflin, 1995. Twins Mickey and Kate Dixon use all of their sleuthing skills when a mysterious shamrock is found on Miss Wink's front door and a strange sign appears on the twins' clubhouse.

VanCleave, Janice. *Microscopes and Magnifying Lenses.* New York: Wiley, 1993. Experiments about clover and other activities using a microscope and/or magnifying lens. Each chapter contains ideas that can be turned into award-winning science fair projects.

———. *Plants.* New York: Wiley, 1997. Experiments about plants. Each chapter contains ideas that can be turned into award-winning science fair projects.

MORE FUN WITH CLOVER!

Make green clover prints to brighten up Saint Patrick's Day. You can make them with three leaves or make your own four-leaf clover. Cut a sponge in the shape of a clover leaf. Moisten the sponge cutout with water, then squeeze out the excess water. Pour a little green tempera paint onto a paper plate. Dip the sponge in the paint, then press it against a sheet of white paper. Repeat to make three or four green clover leaves on the paper. Paint a stem on your clover with an artist's paintbrush.

Spring

30

Spring Equinox

DID YOU KNOW?

On the first day of spring, the hours of daylight and darkness are equal!

From day to day, the length of daylight and darkness changes. The greatest amount of daylight occurs the first day of summer and the least on the first day of winter. In the Northern Hemisphere, summer starts on or about June 21 and winter starts on or about December 22. These dates are called the summer and winter solstice, respectively. On or about March 21 (the first day of spring) and September 23 (the first day of autumn), the amount of daylight and darkness is the same. These dates are called the vernal and autumnal equinox, respectively. (The seasons are reversed in the Southern Hemisphere, with autumn beginning in March, winter in June, spring in September, and summer in December.)

FUN TIME!

Purpose

To show why Earth has different lengths of daylight and darkness during different seasons.

Materials

sharpened pencil
3-inch (7.5-cm) -diameter Styrofoam ball
marker
desk lamp
ruler
adult helper

Procedure

1. Ask an adult to insert the pencil through the Styrofoam ball.
2. Use the marker to draw a line around the center of the Styrofoam ball, to represent the equator.
3. In a darkened room, position the desk lamp so that it shines straight down, with its bulb about 6 inches (15 cm) above the table.
4. Position the ball on the table so that the pencil point is leaning slightly toward the lamp. Observe how much of the ball is lighted up and how much of the ball above and below the equator is not lighted up.
5. Without changing the tilt of the pencil, move the ball around the lamp in a counterclockwise direction. Notice how much of the ball is lighted up. Observe also any changes in the location of the lighted area above and below the equator as the ball is moved.

Results

About half of the ball is lighted up at all times, but the area of the ball that is lighted up changes as the ball moves.

Why?

The ball represents Earth. The pencil is Earth's axis. The sharpened end represents the North Pole, and the eraser the South Pole. The lamp represents the Sun. Moving the ball around the lamp represents Earth's revolving about the Sun. Because Earth is a sphere, the Sun **illuminates** (lights up) half of Earth's surface at any one time.

During the equinoxes, Earth's axis is not tilted toward the Sun, so Earth's illuminated half is from pole to pole, resulting in equal hours of daylight and dark throughout Earth. At the winter solstice in the Northern Hemisphere, the North Pole tilts away from the Sun, resulting in less daylight north of the equator and more daylight south of the equator. The opposite is true at the summer solstice.

BOOK LIST

Noreika, Robert. *A Moon for Seasons.* New York: Simon & Schuster, 1994. Twenty-eight short, expressive poems capture the diverse ways in which the landscape and its inhabitants change with the seasons.

Svedberg, Ulf. *Nicky the Nature Detective.* New York: Farrar, Straus, & Giroux, 1988. A beginning naturalist's guide to the seasons. Describes and explains changes in flora and fauna, while offering lots of exciting ideas for nature activities.

VanCleave, Janice. *Astronomy for Every Kid.* New York: Wiley, 1991. Fun, simple astronomy experiments, including information about equinoxes and solstices.

MORE FUN WITH EQUINOXES!

Some people say that an egg can stand on end at the moment of the vernal or autumnal equinox. Scientists say that an egg that can stand on end could do so at any time. Find out for yourself by trying to balance an egg on end. Do your testing over many days, both before, on, and after the equinox. Consult a newspaper or contact the local television weather station for the exact time of the equinox. Use the same eggs on each day. Make sure you do not keep the eggs out of refrigeration any longer than necessary, and discard the eggs at the end of the experiment. *CAUTION: Wash your hands after handling the eggs because eggs contain bacteria that will make you sick.*

31

Spring Rains

DID YOU KNOW?

Fish have rained from the sky!

The saying "It's raining cats and dogs" is just an expression people use to mean a heavy rain. As far as we know, it is not possible for rain to really contain cats and dogs, but there have been rains containing other small animals, including fish and frogs. In 1947, for example, great numbers of fish rained down on Marksville, Louisiana.

Clouds form when water **evaporates** (changes from a liquid to a vapor) from the surfaces of oceans, lakes, rivers, and other bodies of water, even mud puddles. This vapor condenses on tiny dust particles, forming cloud droplets. When enough droplets get together, they can be seen as clouds. As the cloud droplets bump into each other, they stick together, forming larger drops. Depending on the temperature, the larger drops form either liquid raindrops or solid forms, including **sleet** (frozen raindrops), that fall to Earth's surface. The evaporation of water from Earth and the return of that water either in solid or liquid form is called the **water cycle.**

A possible explanation of how fish might get into a rainstorm is that a **waterspout** (a tornado that touches down on water instead of land) could suck up the fish when it touches down on the water, and then drop them over the land—thus raining fish.

FUN TIME!

Purpose

To demonstrate the water cycle.

Materials

- paper towel
- 16-ounce (480-ml) plastic soda or water bottle with lid
- drinking glass large enough to stand the bottle in
- warm tap water
- ice cube

Procedure

1. Fold the paper towel in half twice.
2. Lay the folded paper towel on a table and stand the glass on it.
3. Fill the bottle half full with warm tap water. Put the lid on the bottle.
4. Invert the bottle and stand it in the glass.
5. Place the ice cube on top of the inverted bottle.
6. Observe the bottle as often as possible for 10 minutes or more, or until the ice melts.

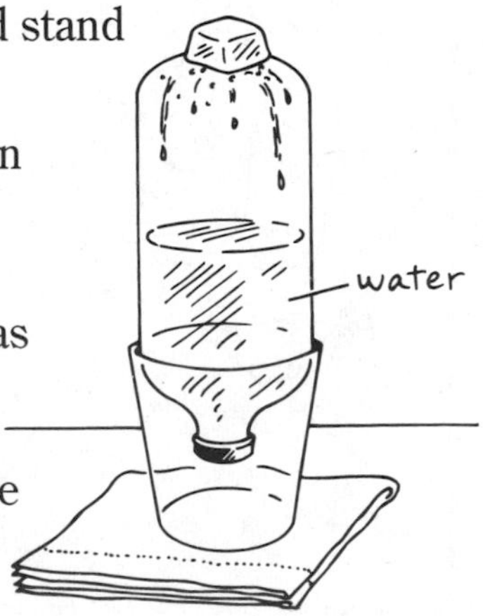

Results

The bottle looks clear at first; then its sides look cloudy as droplets form. As time passes, the tiny droplets combine, forming larger drops. Some of the drops fall and others run down the inside of the bottle.

Why?

Water evaporates from the surface of the warm water, forming water vapor. This water vapor then condenses when it hits the top surface of the bottle or the air beneath, both of which have been cooled by the ice cube. When enough droplets have joined together, they form larger drops that fall down the bottle. This is the same way the water cycle works on Earth.

BOOK LIST

Bauer, Caroline F. *Rainy Day: Stories and Poems.* New York: HarperCollins Children's Books, 1987. A collection of stories and poems about rain by various authors.

Bradley, Franklin Mansfield. *It's Raining Cats and Dogs.* New York: Houghton Mifflin, 1987. Discusses various weather phenomena, including rain, hail, smog, snow, lightning, hurricanes, and tornadoes.

Christian, Spencer. *Can It Really Rain Frogs?* New York: Wiley, 1997. Describes strange weather events such as raining frogs, singing caves, colored rain, and auroras, and discusses weather lore and weather forecasting.

VanCleave, Janice. *Weather.* New York: Wiley, 1995. Experiments about rain and other weather topics. Each chapter contains ideas that can be turned into award-winning science fair projects.

MORE FUN WITH WATER!

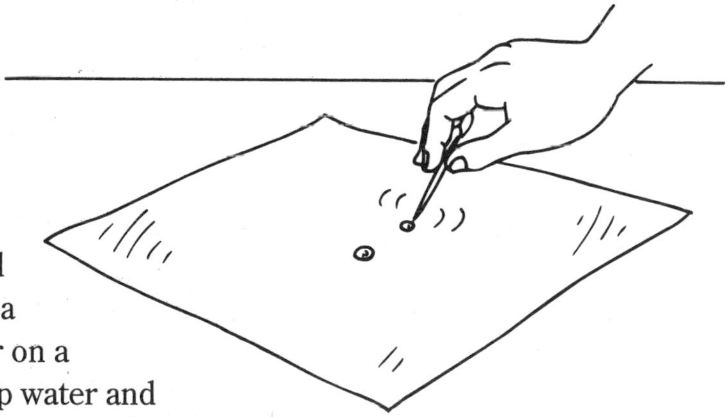

The process by which cloud droplets bump into each other and combine to form raindrops is called **accretion.** Water molecules have an attraction for each other, so when they are near each other, they tend to draw together and combine. See this for yourself. Place a 12-inch (30-cm) piece of waxed paper on a table. Dip your finger into a cup of tap water and allow 3 to 4 drops of water to drop onto the paper about 2 inches (5 cm) apart. Using a toothpick, move one of the water drops toward another drop. Observe what happens when the drops get near each other. Repeat with the remaining water drops.

Spring

32

The Big Dipper

DID YOU KNOW?

The Big Dipper is not a constellation!

The collection of stars we call the Big Dipper is actually an **asterism,** a group of stars that form a shape within a constellation. The Big Dipper forms the lower back and tail of the constellation Ursa Major, the Great Bear. The Big Dipper is generally one of the easiest star patterns to find, but it is especially bright in the spring, when it is found high above the northern horizon.

Because Earth rotates on its axis, stars appear to move in the sky during the night. Imagine the stars on a large sphere surrounding Earth, with Polaris, the North Star, at its northern axis. If you were observing the stars from the North Pole, Polaris would be stationary directly above you and all the other stars would appear to spin around it as Earth rotates. If you moved away from the North Pole, Polaris would appear closer to the northern horizon and only the stars near it would continue to move around in a circle. The stars farther away from Polaris would still make their circular path, but now that path would take them below Earth's horizon and out of sight for part of the night. To an observer on Earth, these stars appear to rise in the east and set in the west. The stars that do not rise or set, but stay above the horizon as they circle the **celestial pole** (a point in the sky above the North or South poles of Earth) are said to be **circumpolar stars.** Polaris is near the north celestial pole. So circumpolar stars in the Northern Hemisphere appear to circle Polaris. The Big Dipper stars in Ursa Major are circumpolar at about latitude 40°N and farther north.

FUN TIMES!

Purpose

To locate the Big Dipper and Ursa Major in the spring.

Materials

directional compass

Procedure

1. During the day, use the compass to determine the direction north.
2. Find a place that provides the best view of the northern part of the sky.
3. On a clear, moonless night, go outside and stand in the designated spot, facing north.
4. Look for seven stars that form the shapes of a large dipper. (Note that in spring the dipper is upside down, so the bear is also upside down. Turn this book upside down to see how the dipper and the bear appear in the spring sky.)
5. Using the Big Dipper as a guide, look for the other stars that make up Ursa Major.

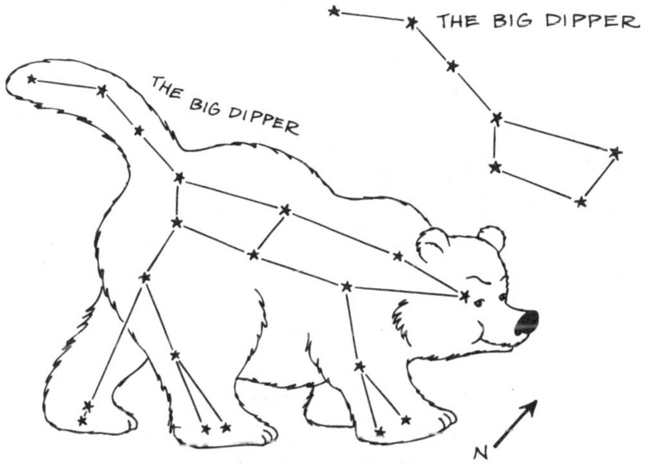

Results

You should be able to see the Big Dipper as well as some or all of the stars of Ursa Major.

Why?

The stars of Ursa Major are not always easy to find, but using the Big Dipper as a guide can help you locate them. It is easiest to find in the spring when it is high above the horizon.

BOOK LIST

Krupp, Edwin C. *The Big Dipper and You.* New York: William Morrow, 1989. Presents what is known today and past beliefs about the Big Dipper, and gives added information on the North Star, Polaris.

Mosley, John. *The Ultimate Guide to the Sky.* Los Angeles: Lowell House, 1997. Created especially for kids to use on their own, this easy-to-use guide features descriptions of 88 constellations, listed alphabetically. It also has easy-to-read star maps for each month of the year and a listing of tools that beginning astronomers need.

Rey, Hans Augusto. *Find the Constellations.* New York: Houghton Mifflin, 1989. Describes stars and constellations throughout the year and offers ways of identifying them.

VanCleave, Janice. *Astronomy for Every Kid.* New York: Wiley, 1991. Fun, simple experiments about astronomy, including information about the Big Dipper.

———. *Constellations for Every Kid.* New York: Wiley, 1997. Fun, simple constellation experiments, including information about the Big Dipper and Ursa Major.

MORE FUN WITH STARS!

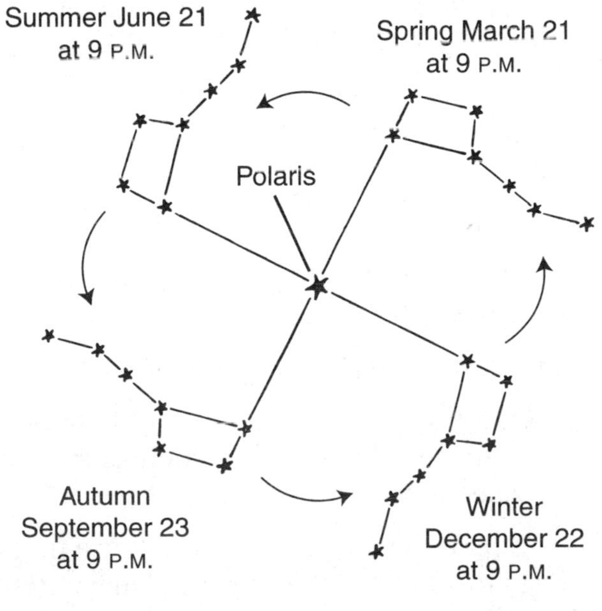

The Big Dipper can be used during any season to locate Polaris. Just line up the two stars that form the outer edge of the bowl of the dipper and extend the imaginary line beyond the bowl. The next star you see is Polaris. (Note that Polaris is not a very bright star.) The star map here shows how the Big Dipper can be used to locate Polaris on the first day of each season at 9:00 P.M. But during the night from one hour to the next, or at the same time of night from one season to the next, the asterism moves in a counterclockwise direction around Polaris. Regardless of the position of the Big Dipper, its stars continue to point to Polaris.

33

Earth Day

DID YOU KNOW?

The average American family of four throws away about 5,000 pounds (2,273 kg) of trash each year!

About 73 percent of our trash is buried in **landfills** (low areas built up from deposits of solid trash), 14 percent is burned in **incinerators** (furnaces for burning trash) to produce energy, and 13 percent is recycled. Many things, such as plastics, will be in landfills for many hundreds of years because it takes them so long to decay.

What can you do to solve this problem? The most important thing is to remember these three R's: reduce, reuse, recycle. First, *reduce* the amount of trash you throw away. Use disposable items sparingly. For example, use only one paper towel if that is all that is needed to do the job. Second, *reuse* items as many times as possible. For example, you can keep bits of string, ribbon, and paper from presents for craft projects instead of throwing them away. Third, *recycle* things such as metal cans and buy things made from recycled materials. Recycled objects are collected and reprocessed into new, usable items.

Earth Day is celebrated each year on April 22. It is a time when schools, communities, and individuals pull together to improve the environment by cleaning up public places and planting trees and flowers. This day serves to remind us to take care of our planet. But we need to remember the Earth Day motto, which is "Make every day Earth Day."

FUN TIME!

Purpose

To discover how much of your trash is packaging.

Materials

masking tape
marker
3 trash bags
rubber gloves
adult helper

Procedure

1. Using the tape and marker, label the trash bags WET, DRY, and OTHER.
2. For 1 day or longer, collect and separate everything your family usually throws away into the 3 bags as follows:

   Trash from Packaging Items

   - WET throwaway packaging, such as milk cartons, food cans, soda cans, and plastic bottles.
   - DRY throwaway packaging, such as cake boxes, plastic bags, and food wrappers.

   Trash from Nonpackaging Items

   - OTHER—Anything that would not be considered packaging, such as magazines, apple cores, and used paper towels.
3. Compare the amount of trash in the first 2 bags to what's in the last bag. How much of your trash is packaging?

4. Now, wearing rubber gloves and with adult assistance, sort through all the bags for items that can be reused or recycled. Contact your local department of public works for information on recycling in your area.

Results

The total volume of your 2 bags of packaging materials probably held more than the bag of nonpackaging.

Why?

A longer period of time would be needed to make an accurate estimate of the amount of your trash that is packaging. Although packaging is crushed at landfills, it makes up about 30 percent by volume of the average American's family trash.

Packaging has some important uses, such as keeping food clean, protecting it from being crushed, and giving information and instructions about the product. But there is often more packaging than is necessary. Here are some tips for cutting down on packaging: Take your lunch in a reusable container instead of a throwaway bag. Reuse plastic grocery bags or use a cloth bag to carry your purchases. Buy food in bulk rather than in individually wrapped pieces.

BOOK LIST

Gardner, Robert. *Celebrating Earth Day.* Brookfield, CT: Millbrook Press, 1992. Celebrates Earth Day by suggesting activities and experiments for learning more about Earth and how to improve its condition.

Levine, Shari. *Projects for a Healthy Planet.* New York: Wiley, 1992. Simple experiments about helping the environment, including several on reducing waste.

VanCleave, Janice. *Ecology for Every Kid.* New York: Wiley, 1996. Fun, simple ecology experiments, including information about trash.

MORE FUN WITH TRASH!

Reuse an empty box, such as a cake box, by making a monster trash chomper. Wrap the box in plain waste paper, and secure with transparent tape. Wrap a piece of masking tape around the middle of the box. Wrap a second strip of tape around the box, next to the first strip of tape. Use a marker to draw teeth on the tape, making jagged lines as shown. Ask an adult to use a knife to cut across the box between the rows of teeth, stopping at one of the narrow sides of the box. Use crayons and/or markers to draw the face of a monster trash chomper on the box. Holding the top of the box, open and close its bottom to make your chomper chomp. Your monster trash chomper feeds on litter, which is bits of scrap paper or other trash scattered around your house. Feed the monster by picking up the litter.

34

Conserving Paper

DID YOU KNOW?

Using "chewed paper" helps conserve natural resources!

Most paper is made from wood **pulp** (a soft, moist, slightly sticky material used to make paper). The pulp is made by grinding trees into small pieces, mixing the pieces with water and other chemicals, and cooking the whole mess. The pulp is then pressed into flat sheets of paper. Trees commonly used to make paper are spruce, fir, hemlock, poplar, pine, tamarack, and many hardwoods.

Recycled paper is made by de-inking and shredding used paper and blending the pieces with water. The resulting pulp is pressed into newsprint, cardboard boxes, paper bags, and other paper products. The energy used to reprocess waste materials may be far less than that required for making new materials. So in addition to saving trees, making recycled paper takes much less energy than producing an equal amount of paper from trees. But the cost of recycled paper is often not less than that of regular paper because other costs are involved, including the costs of collecting and transporting used paper.

One way to reuse paper is to make papier-mâché, which literally means "chewed paper" in French. Papier-mâché can be used for art and science projects, such as making models.

FUN TIME!

Purpose

To try a method of reusing paper.

Materials

2 sheets of newspaper
electric food blender
2 cups (500 ml) tap water
large tea strainer
1-quart (1-liter) bowl
2 tablespoons (30 ml) school glue
1-quart (1-liter) resealable plastic bag
adult helper

Procedure

1. Tear the sheets of newspaper into small pieces.
2. Place the pieces of newspaper in the blender and add the water.
3. With adult supervision, turn on the blender and thoroughly mix the paper and water until a thick mixture is produced. This is your pulp.
4. Pour the pulp into the tea strainer and allow as much water to drain out as possible. Lightly press against the pulp, squeezing out excess water, but do not press it into a hard, waterless mass.
5. Pour the pulp into the bowl.

6. Add the glue and mix thoroughly with your hands.
7. Use the mixture to make beads (see "More Fun with Paper" below) or models. If you are not going to use the mixture right away, you can store it in the plastic bag in the refrigerator.

Results

You have made papier-mâché.

Why?

Papier-mâché is a mixture of paper and glue that can be used to make jewelry, masks, animal models, and much more.

BOOK LIST

McGraw, Sheila. *Papier-Mâché for Kids.* Buffalo, NY: Firefly Books, 1991. Step-by-step easy instructions show how to make papier-mâché pigs, cats, masks, monsters, and more. Eight great projects in all.

VanCleave, Janice. *Ecology for Every Kid.* New York: Wiley, 1996. Fun, simple ecology experiments, including information about conserving natural resources

MORE FUN WITH PAPER!

To make beads from papier-mâché, press some of the mixture around a pencil. Shape the bead, then carefully slip it off the pencil and place it on a cookie sheet. To make beads with smaller holes, press the papier-mâché mixture around a knitting needle or wooden skewer. Allow the beads to air-dry for 1 day or more. If you want the beads to dry quickly, ask an adult to help you place the cookie sheet in an oven at 200°F (93°C) for 1 hour or until the beads are dry, and then to remove the pan and allow the beads to cool. Paint the dry beads with tempera paint, then string the bigger beads on colored yarn and the smaller ones on string.

35

Hummers

DID YOU KNOW?

Hummingbirds never walk or hop!

There are about 319 species of hummingbirds, and they only live in the **Western Hemisphere** (region of Earth consisting mainly of North and South America). The largest is the South American giant hummingbird, which is 8½ inches (21.3 cm) long, while the smallest (also the smallest bird in the world) is the Cuban bee hummingbird, which is 2¼ inches (5.6 cm) long. The name "hummingbird" comes from the humming sound made by their wings. The wings hum because they are moving so quickly—in some of the birds, about 60 to 70 times a second. This means that in the time it takes you to say "one thousand and one," a hummingbird can flap its wings 60 to 70 times.

A hummingbird's feet are small and weak. It uses them to perch on branches or other objects, but never to walk or hop, even for short distances. Hummingbirds also have interesting beaks and eating habits. A hummingbird's beak is long and hollow and holds a long tongue that curls over at the edges to form a tube. Hummingbirds use this tubular tongue to suck up **nectar** (sugary liquid) from flowers.

FUN TIME!

Purpose

To observe the feeding habits of hummingbirds.

Materials

spoon
3 cups (750 ml) tap water
1 cup (250 ml) sugar
1-quart (1-liter) jar with lid
red food coloring
hummingbird feeder (found in stores that sell pet supplies)
field guide to birds
adult helper

Procedure

1. Mix the water and sugar in the jar.
2. Add 20 drops of food coloring to make the sugar water red. Stir.
3. Fill the bottle of the feeder and secure its feeding base.
4. Ask an adult to hang the feeder near a window where it can be observed from inside your home.
5. Observe the feeder as often as possible for 2 weeks or more. Make note of the behavior of the hummingbirds as they feed. Use a field guide or other book to identify the hummingbirds by their appearance and behavior.

Results

Hummingbirds will hover in front of the feeder and sip the sugar water. Generally, more young birds are attracted to a feeder that has just been hung. Some of the birds may seem more cautious and nervous, while others appear more calm.

WHY?

Some scientists think that all hummingbirds are attracted to the color red, but others think that only the young birds are attracted. Either way, red food coloring is often added to hummingbird food to attract the birds. Young birds are very curious and will investigate anything. That may be why they are more attracted to the red feeder. Older birds vary in behavior. Some may be cautious and nervous because this is their nature, while others approach the feeder with complete assurance. You can identify a male by his **iridescent** (shiny rainbow-like colored) throat feathers.

BOOK LIST

Iverson, Carol. *Hummingbirds Can Fly Backwards, and Other Facts and Curiosities.* Minneapolis, MN: Lerner, 1991. A collection of miscellaneous facts about nature, animals, plants, and the human body.

Rauzon, Mark. *Hummingbirds.* Danbury, CT: Franklin Watts, 1997. Describes the physical characteristics, behavior, and habitat of the smallest bird in the world.

VanCleave, Janice. *Animals.* New York: Wiley, 1993. Experiments about birds and other animals. Each chapter contains ideas that can be turned into award-winning science fair projects.

MORE FUN WITH HUMMINGBIRDS!

It is believed that hummingbirds can distinguish all the colors. They may be particularly attracted to red because it stands out against background foliage. Discover for yourself if the hummingbirds that visit your feeder prefer a specific color. Once the feeder with red water has been in place long enough to attract hummingbirds, change the color of the water to blue. Observe the feeder with blue water for 2 weeks to determine if there has been any change in the number of birds visiting the feeder. Experiment with other colors of water as well as using no coloring in the water. Refill and clean feeder as needed.

36

Early Risers

DID YOU KNOW?

Morning glories wake with the morning sun!

Although they don't actually sleep, morning glories do open in the morning and close at night. Chemicals in the plants cause an increase in **turgor pressure** (pressure caused by water inside a plant cell) in the presence of light. The increase in turgor pressure causes the morning glory petals to open. Plant movement due to turgor pressure is called **turgor movement.**

Turgor pressure also causes a plant to stand upright. When a plant receives the proper amount of water, its cells are full of water and firm, so the plant's stems are firm. But if the plant does not receive enough water, it uses up the water in its cells and they become soft, causing the plant to wilt (droop).

FUN TIME!

Purpose

To show how water moves through a plant.

Materials

stalk of celery
juice glass
red food coloring
scissors

Procedure

1. Stand the celery in the glass for 3 hours or until the celery wilts.
2. Remove the celery and fill the glass about half full with water.
3. Add enough food coloring to make the water a deep red color.
4. Use the scissors to cut across the bottom of the celery stem.
5. Hold the celery stalk and bend it back and forth without breaking it to determine how firm it is.
6. Stand the celery in the glass of colored water.
7. Observe the leaves immediately and each day for 2 days.
8. Repeat step 5.

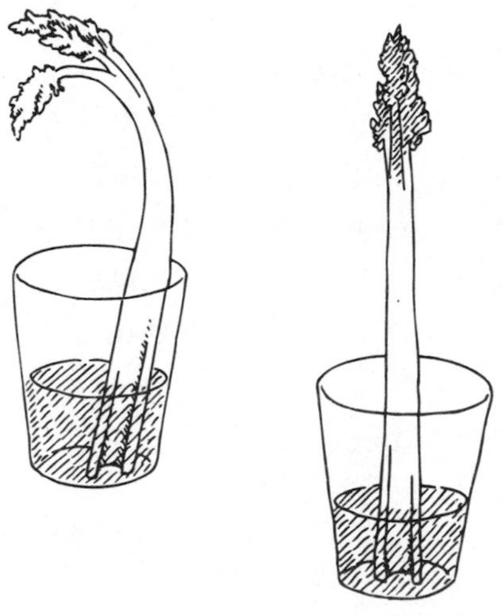

Results

The celery leaves turn from green to reddish green. The stalk changes from soft and bendable to firm and crisp.

Why?

The wilted celery did not have enough water in its cells to make the cells firm. The red water moved up the stalk through transport tubes, filling the cells and causing the celery stalk to become firm. After a while due to turgor pressure, the celery stalk becomes firm and stands upright.

BOOK LIST

Johnson, Sylvia A. *Morning Glories.* Minneapolis, MN: Lerner, 1985. Examines the lives of morning glories and the stages of development leading to the production of their delicate flowers.

Pohl, Kathleen. *Morning Glories.* Austin, TX: Raintree, 1990. Describes in text and photographs the life cycle of the morning glory.

VanCleave, Janice. *Plants.* New York: Wiley, 1997. Experiments about turgor pressure and other plant topics. Each chapter contains ideas that can be turned into award-winning science fair projects.

MORE FUN WITH TURGOR PRESSURE!

Show how morning glories open when their petals fill with water. Lay a sheet of white unlined paper over the flower pattern shown here and trace the flower with a pencil. Cut out the tracing. Fold each petal toward the middle along the fold lines. Fill a large bowl about half full with water. Hold the folded paper flower, petal side up, about 4 inches (10 cm) above the bowl. Drop the flower into the bowl and watch the petals. You may wish to design your own flower, changing the number and shape of the petals. Another thing to discover is how different kinds of paper affect the speed at which the paper petals open. Try newspaper and construction paper.

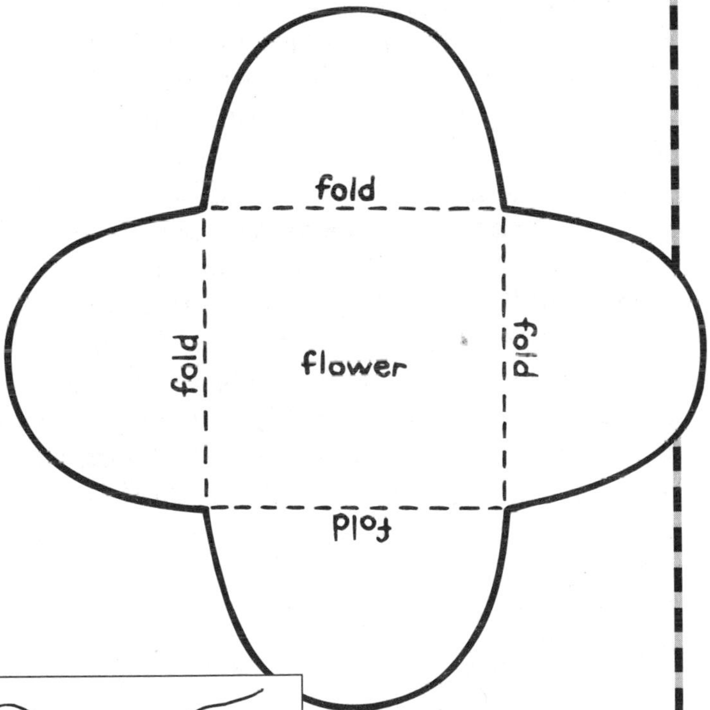

Spring

37

Dinnertime

DID YOU KNOW?

Flies taste with their feet!

Insects have taste organs, which are usually located on their mouthparts. But some insects, such as houseflies, can taste with their feet. As flies walk on food, **nerves** (bundles of cells that send messages throughout the body) in the taste organs detect the presence of different chemicals in the food and send a message to the fly's brain.

Human **saliva** (a liquid containing chemicals that digest some foods), like that of flies and many other insects, contains a chemical called **amylase.** Amylase digests **starch,** a complex chemical found in many foods, into less complex chemicals. When flies drop saliva on food, the amylase in the saliva quickly begins to digest the starch in the food, forming a liquid that the fly can eat. The **proboscis** (feeding tube) of most flies has a sponge-like tip. The spongy tip soaks up liquids, then the fly sucks the liquids into its body through the proboscis.

FUN TIME!

Purpose

To demonstrate how flies eat.

Materials

firm cookie (such as chocolate chip)
glass of milk

Procedure

1. Dip the edge of the cookie into the milk.
2. Place the wet end of the cookie in your mouth and suck the milk from it.

Results

Along with the liquid, you suck up some of the softened cookie.

Why?

Flies don't have teeth with which to chew their food, but the chemicals in their saliva break food into small parts. When the small parts dissolve in the saliva, the flies can suck up the liquid food.

BOOK LIST

Berger, Melvin. *Flies Taste with Their Feet.* New York: Scholastic Paperbacks, 1997. Weird facts about insects.

Branzei, Sylvia. *Grossology: The Science of Creatures Gross and Disgusting.* New York: Penguin, 1996. An icky concoction of memorable scientific facts, including how a fly eats, the amount of saliva different animals make per day, and lots of other gross stuff.

Knapp, Ron. *Blood Suckers.* Springfield, NJ: Enslow, 1996. Mosquitoes, fleas, lice, leeches, and vampire bats are the common bloodsucking creatures featured.

VanCleave, Janice. *Insects and Spiders.* New York: Wiley, 1999. Experiments about flies and other insects as well as spiders. Each chapter contains ideas that can be turned into award-winning science fair projects.

MORE FUN WITH FLIES!

Another type of fly is the mosquito. Mosquitoes have an elongated sucking proboscis with which to eat. A mosquito that feeds on blood stabs your skin with its sharp proboscis and sucks out the blood. Only females are blood feeders. Both males and females feed on flower nectar. Here's a way to demonstrate how a mosquito eats. Cover the top of a glass of fruit juice with aluminum foil. Holding the foil in place, tilt the straw and push the end through the foil covering. Drink some of the juice through the straw.

Water Walkers

DID YOU KNOW?

Some animals can walk on water!

The tendency of molecules of a liquid, such as water, to cling together at the surface forming a skin-like film, is called **surface tension.** Because water has surface tension, lightweight bugs can walk across the surface without sinking.

Insects do not have feet like yours. Instead, the legs of most adult insects end in a pair of claws with usually one or more pad-like structures between them. The pads between the claws of flies are covered with moist hairs that allow the flies to walk on the ceiling or on slippery surfaces.

FUN TIME!

Purpose

To demonstrate how insects walk on water.

Materials

scissors
ruler
corrugated cardboard (from a box)
one 12-inch (30-cm) cotton terry stem (special pipe cleaner available at craft stores) *or* chenille craft stem (available at craft stores) with a thin layer of petroleum jelly on them
marker
large see-through bowl
tap water

Procedure

1. Cut a 3-by-1-inch (7.5-by-2.5-cm) strip from the cardboard, cutting the 3-inch (7.5-cm) sides across the grooves. This strip will be the body of the insect.
2. Cut notches in the strip to shape the body into three parts. The middle body part should have three grooves.
3. Cut three 4-inch (10-cm) pieces from the cotton terry stem.
4. Stick each piece of stem all the way through the three grooves in the middle part of the insect's body so that the same amount of stem sticks out on either side. The stems will be the insect's legs.
5. Draw two eyes on the insect's head.
6. Bend each leg down where it meets the insect's body. Then bend about ¼ inch (0.6 cm) of the end of each leg out to shape a foot. Stand the insect on a table and adjust the bends in the legs so that each foot touches the table.

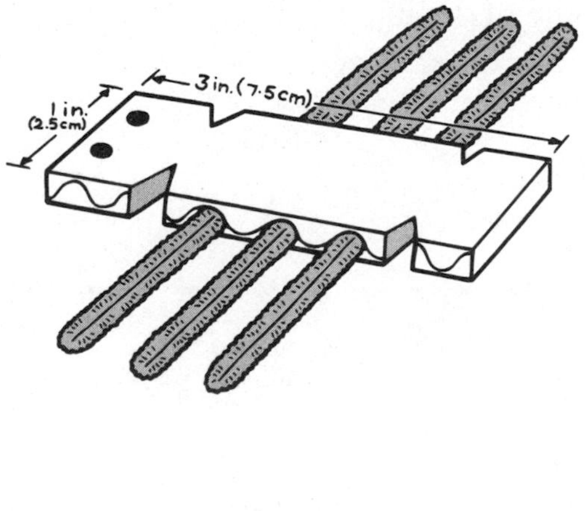

7. Fill the bowl three-fourths full with water.

8. Slowly lower the insect into the water until its feet touch the surface, then release it.

Results

The insect stands on the water's surface.

Why?

The cardboard insect, like real insects, can stand on the water's surface because of the surface tension of water.

BOOK LIST

Kneidel, Sally. *More Pet Bugs.* New York: Wiley, 1999. Fun bug experiments, including information about water-walking insects called water striders.

Mound, Laurence. *Insects.* Eyewitness Books. New York: Knopf, 1990. Photos and descriptions of different insects, including information about water bugs.

VanCleave, Janice. *Insects and Spiders.* New York: Wiley, 1999. Experiments about insects' feet and other insect and spider topics. Each chapter contains ideas that can be turned into award-winning science fair projects.

MORE FUN WITH INSECTS!

The ends of the moist hairs on a fly's feet wet the surface the insect walks on. The wet hairs then stick to the wet surface. Demonstrate this type of holding power by making a paper model of a fly. Cut a 2-inch (5-cm) -square piece of paper and fold it in half. Use the pattern shown to draw half of an insect on the paper. Cut out the insect, cutting through both layers of paper.

Open the paper, bend the legs down, then bend the end of the paper legs to shape the insect's feet. Wet the feet with water. Hold a saucer upright and touch the wet feet to the saucer's outside bottom. Release the paper. The paper feet should stick to the saucer so that the insect hangs upside down from the saucer.

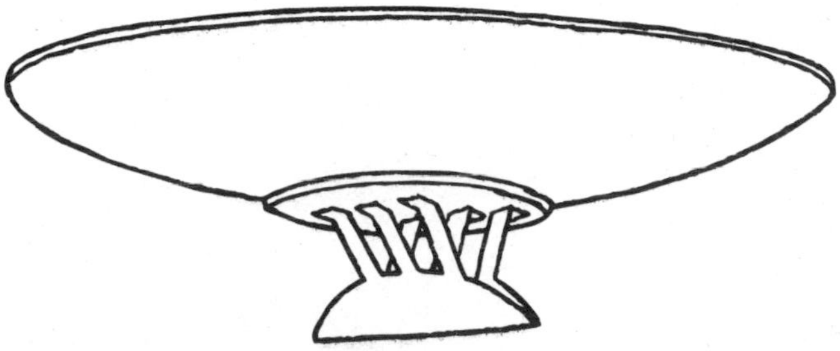

Frog Bite

DID YOU KNOW?

Frogs have teeth, but they don't chew!

When spring comes, frogs come out of hibernation. Their increased activity requires more energy, so they begin to eat. Frogs are **carnivores** (meat eaters), like most other adult amphibians. **Amphibians** are animals, such as frogs, toads, and salamanders, which are cold-blooded, live part of their lives in water and part on land, and do not have hair, scales, or feathers. The diet of frogs is mainly insects, but they will eat most anything that moves and is small enough to swallow whole.

The frog has a long tongue that can extend far out of its mouth. Prey get stuck to a sticky secretion on the end of the frog's tongue, and then the frog draws the prey into its mouth. Small, cone-shaped teeth in the roof of the mouth are used to hold prey but are not used for biting or chewing.

FUN TIME!

Purpose

To make a model of a frog's tongue.

Materials

party blower
12 self-sticking Velcro circles (found with sewing needs in department stores)
pencil
ruler
sheet of unruled white paper
scissors

Procedure

1. Unwind the party blower and attach a hooked Velcro circle to the end. (Note that Velcro has two parts, one that has hooks and the other loops. The looped part looks more fuzzy.) Set the 11 remaining hooked Velcro circles aside.
2. Draw twelve 1-inch (2.5-cm) -long ovals on the paper to represent insects.
3. Cut out the paper insects, and attach a looped Velcro circle to each.
4. Spread the insects on a table with the Velcro side faceup.
5. Blow through the party blower, touching the end to an insect.
6. Remove the insect from the end of the party blower and repeat step 5 to catch the other insects.

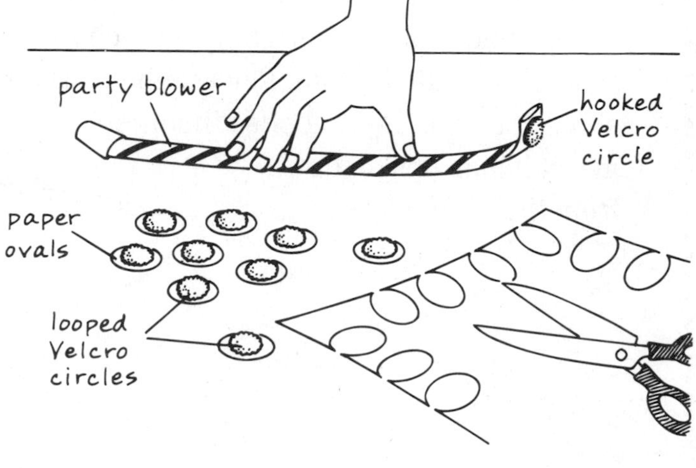

Results

The paper insect sticks to the sticky end of the party blower. When the party blower rewinds, the paper insect is drawn toward your mouth.

Why?

The party blower represents a frog's tongue. When the frog sees prey, it quickly unrolls its tongue so that the sticky end of the tongue hits the insect. If the insect is hit, it gets stuck on the sticky part of the frog's tongue the same way the Velcro insect stuck to the Velcro on the party blower. Then the frog brings its tongue back into its mouth and eats its meal.

BOOK LIST

Gibbons, Gail. *Frogs.* New York: Holiday House, 1993. Presents interesting facts about frogs, including how their bodies change as they grow from tadpoles into frogs, how they make sounds that can mean different things, how they hibernate, and how they differ from toads.

Lewis, Beverly. *Frog Power.* Minneapolis, MN: Bethany House, 1995. Stacy Henry hates frogs—especially Jason Birchall's pet bullfrog, Croaker. When she plans an Easter pet parade, she's sure Jason's frog will spoil it. Are her concerns justified?

Lovett, Sarah. *Extremely Weird Frogs.* Santa Fe, NM: John Muir, 1996. Describes the habitat, appearance, and behavior of a variety of unusual frogs.

Patent, Dorothy Hinshaw. *Flashy Fantastic Rain Forest Frogs.* New York: Scholastic, 1997. An informative book with beautiful colored illustrations of the bright blue, red, orange, and pink rain forest frogs.

VanCleave, Janice. *Animals.* New York: Wiley, 1993. Experiments about frogs and other animals. Each chapter contains ideas that can be turned into award-winning science fair projects.

MORE FUN WITH FROGS' TONGUES!

Use frog's-tongue party blowers and one of the paper insects to play a game. Make a frog's-tongue party blower for each player. Tape one end of a 30-inch (75-cm) string to the center of a doorway. Hang the paper insect from the free end of the string by attaching it with tape. One at a time, let each player try to catch the hanging insect using his or her frog's tongue. Remove the caught insect from the tongue and try again. Each capture of the insect scores one point. How many points can you score in five tries?

Summer

In summer, the tilt of Earth toward the Sun brings high temperatures and long days. Try counting cricket chirps to determine the temperature. Discover how sunscreen protects your skin from the Sun's damaging ultraviolet light, why light-colored clothes keep you cool, and why your fingers and toes wrinkle when you swim.

DATES TO MARK ON YOUR CALENDAR

- *June 16, 1963,* is the date Soviet cosmonaut Valentina Tereshkova became the first woman in space.
- *On or about June 21* is the summer solstice, the first day of summer and the longest day of the year.
- *July 12, 1864,* is the birth date of George Washington Carver, an African American biologist who experimented with peanuts and sweet potatoes.
- *From July 15 to August 15,* look for the Delta Aquariad meteor shower. July 29 and August 2 are the best nights to observe.
- *July 20, 1969,* is the day that Neil Armstrong became the first human being to set foot on the Moon.
- *July 22, 1822,* is the birth date of Gregor Johann Mendel, an Austrian monk who was the first person to discover the basic laws of heredity and suggest the existence of genes.
- *July 23 to August 20* are the dates when you can view the Perseid meteor shower, with August 12 being the best night to observe.
- *July 30, 1863,* is the birth date of Henry Ford, the man who founded the Ford Motor Company, which manufactured some of the very first cars.
- *On August 12, 1887,* Thomas Alva Edison, reciting a nursery rhyme, made the first sound recording on his Edisonphone.
- *August 27, 1883,* is the day that Krakatoa volcano in Indonesia erupted. It was the most violent explosion on Earth in modern times and was heard 3,000 miles (4,800 km) away.

40

Color Changers

DID YOU KNOW?

Chameleons cannot change every color!

Chameleons can change many colors, and even patterns, but not every color. For example, a chameleon can't change color to shocking pink, or plaid! Chameleons' color changes help them blend in with their background. This doesn't mean that they look at their surroundings and make a decision to change color to match it. Instead, their color changes come about because of changes in light intensity, temperature, or emotional state.

Under the outer, transparent skin of a chameleon are layers of skin (cells containing pigment). The first layer contains **chromatophores,** yellow and red pigments. Under this layer are two reflective layers, one reflecting blue light and the other white light. Next is a layer of chromatophores with dark brown pigment called **melanin.** The color of a chameleon's skin is actually a combination of colors. To change the color of the skin, the color cells alter in size, so that by variation of the amounts of yellow, red, and dark brown pigments, different colors are produced. The reflecting layers also cause color changes. For example, when the blue layer is under cells containing yellow pigment, green is produced. The color change can be caused by nerves, which results in a quick change, and by chemicals carried to the color cells, which is slower (taking about 1 minute).

FUN TIME!

Purpose

To determine how chameleons change color.

Materials

2 sheets of colored plastic—1 blue, 1 yellow
fine-point black permanent marker

Procedure

1. Lay the blue sheet of plastic on the drawing of the chameleon.
2. Lay the yellow sheet of plastic over the blue plastic. Observe the color change of the chameleon.

Results

The chameleon changes from blue to green.

Why?

Light reflecting off the blue and yellow plastic blends together, producing green light. In a similar way, when light reflects off the blue reflective layer of a chameleon's skin and blends with the yellow pigment in the upper layer, the chameleon looks green.

BOOK LIST

de Vosjoli, Philippe. *Green Anoles.* Santee, CA: Advanced Vivarium Systems, 1992. The general care and maintenance of green anoles.

Mara, H. P. *Chameleons.* Capstone, 1998. Describes the physical characteristics, habitat, and behavior of the chameleon.

VanCleave, Janice. *Animals.* New York: Wiley, 1993. Experiments about chameleons and other animals. Each chapter contains ideas that can be turned into award-winning science fair projects.

Walton, Marilyn Jeffers. *Chameleon's Rainbow.* Austin, TX: Raintree/Steck-Vaughn, 1993. Two chameleons, Chauncy and Winston, set out to fool a cranky old vulture who has stolen both their rainbow and their pot of gold.

Zoffer, David J. *Feeding Insect-Eating Lizards.* Neptune City, NJ: T. F. H. Publications, 1994. Information on the care of lizards, including anoles. Includes details on housing and nutrition.

MORE FUN WITH LIZARDS!

An **anole** is a **reptile** (a cold-blooded vertebrate that breathes with lungs and has dry, scaly, or horny skin) that is closely related to the chameleon. Anoles also change color, but mostly shades of brown and green. Consider having an anole for a pet. First, be sure you are prepared to take care of it. You'll need the right **habitat** (natural surroundings of living things) and a commitment to feed and care for the anole. Read about anoles and prepare a proper habitat before purchasing your pet. Your local pet store can provide more information. Once your pet has become familiar with its new surroundings, make observations to determine what causes it to change color.

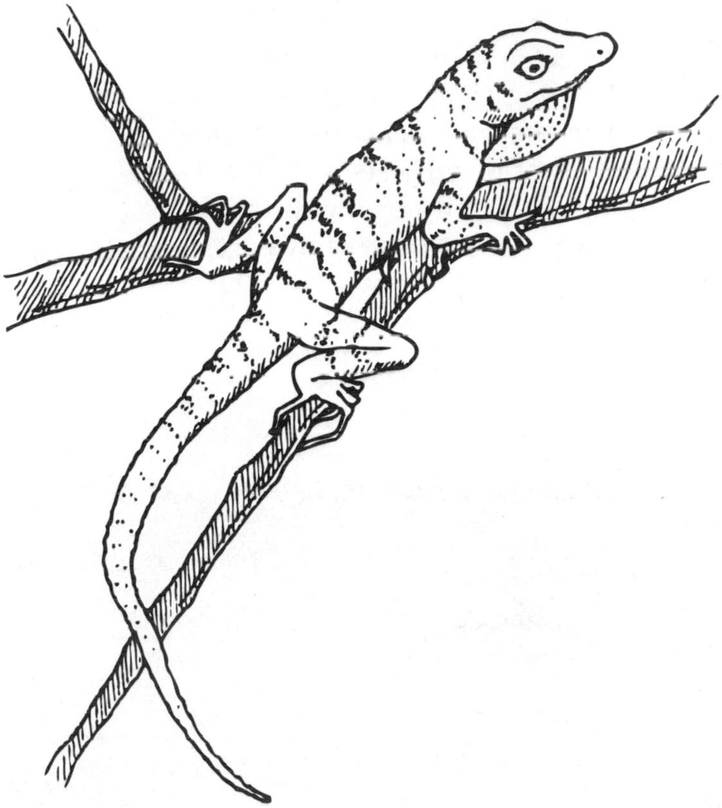

41

Critters' Ears

DID YOU KNOW?

Crickets have "ears" on their legs!

A cricket's "ear" is a thin, flexible skin, called a **tympanic membrane,** located on its leg. You have a tympanic membrane inside your ear, called an eardrum. The cricket's tympanic membrane, like yours, vibrates when **sound waves** (vibrations traveling through air or another material) strike it. Nerves send a message to the brain that the tympanic membrane is vibrating, and the brain decodes the vibrations.

Many insects make sounds, but only a few of these sounds, including those made by crickets, can be heard by people. The sound made by crickets is called chirping. Crickets chirp by **stridulation,** which involves rubbing one body part against another.

FUN TIME!

Purpose

To demonstrate how crickets make sounds.

Materials

transparent tape
index card
fingernail file or emery board

Procedure

1. Tape one of the long sides of the index card to a table.
2. Holding the corner of the other long side of the card, lift that side about 2 inches (5 cm) off the table.
3. Slowly move the fingernail file back and forth across the raised edge of the card. Observe the sound produced.
4. Repeat step 3, this time moving the file quickly.

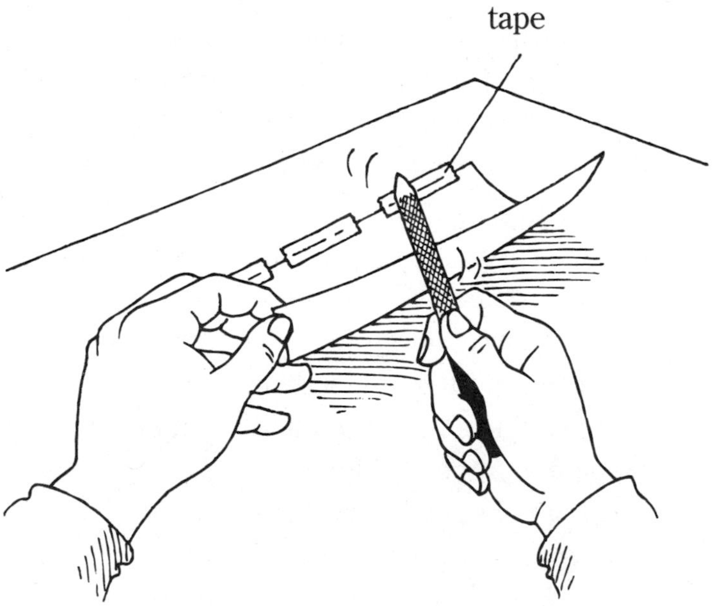

Results

A sound is produced. The faster you move the file, the higher the sound's **pitch** (high or low quality of a sound).

Why?

A sound is produced when a rough surface is rubbed against the sharp edge of something. In the male cricket, the rough part of one wing is rubbed against the sharp edge of another wing. As with the nail file, the faster the wings move, the higher the pitch of the sound produced.

BOOK LIST

DuBosque, Doug C. *Draw Insects.* Columbus, NC: Peel Productions, 1997. The fun world of insects comes to life with accurate drawings, clear instructions, and amazing scientific information about crickets and other insects.

Johnson, Sylvia A. *Chirping Insects.* Minneapolis, MN: Lerner, 1986. Describes how chirping insects such as crickets, katydids, and grasshoppers produce their songs and use them to send messages to other members of their species.

Kneidel, Sally. *Pet Bugs.* New York: Wiley, 1994. An interesting book on how to catch and keep crickets, as well as other interesting bugs, as pets.

VanCleave, Janice. *Insects and Spiders.* New York: Wiley, 1999. Experiments about crickets and other insects as well as spiders. Each chapter contains ideas that can be turned into award-winning science fair projects.

MORE FUN WITH CRICKETS

Temperature affects the rate at which a male cricket chirps. As the temperature increases, the chirping rate increases. A cricket's chirping rate can be used to determine the temperature of the air. How accurate a thermometer is a cricket?

Catch a male cricket or purchase one at a pet store. (Male and female crickets can be identified by looking at their hind end. They both have two feelers, but the female has a third tube that looks like a stinger—it is actually an egg-laying tube called an **ovipositor.**) Place the cricket in a jar and stretch a piece of nylon stocking over the mouth of the jar. Secure the stocking with a rubber band. Count the number of cricket chirps you hear in 15 seconds. Then add 40 to the number of chirps. This will be the temperature in degrees Fahrenheit. Repeat the process three times. Average the results by adding the totals and dividing by 4. Release the cricket outdoors after you have finished.

42

Summer Smells

DID YOU KNOW?

Warm things have more smell!

Smell happens inside your nose. The "chocolate" smell of a candy bar comes from particles that leave the candy and enter the air. When air containing these particles enters your nose, the particles are picked up by special smell-detecting cells in your nose. These detectors send a message to your brain telling you that chocolate is nearby.

Odor is the property of a substance that activates the smell detectors. Materials give off odor as soon as particles on their surface **vaporize,** or change to a vapor. The more vapor that enters the nose at one time, the stronger the smell. The warmer the material, the more it vaporizes and the more its odor gets into your nose. Very cold materials vaporize so little that they have little or no odor.

FUN TIME!

Purpose

To demonstrate the effect of temperature on smell.

Materials

4 tablespoons (120 ml) chocolate ice cream
two 5-ounce (150-ml) paper cups
timer

Procedure

1. Place 2 tablespoons (60 ml) of ice cream in each cup.
2. Place one cup in the freezer and leave the other cup sitting at room temperature.
3. When the ice cream in the cup at room temperature is melted and warm, which will take about 15 minutes, smell its contents.
4. Take the cup from the freezer and smell its contents. Compare the smell of the frozen ice cream to that of the melted ice cream.

Results

The warm, melted ice cream has a stronger chocolate smell.

Why?

The warmer a material, the more its particles vaporize and enter your hose. More chocolate particles of the warm ice cream enter your nose and are picked up by your smell detectors.

BOOK LIST

Cobb, Vicki. *How to Really Fool Yourself: Illusions for All Your Senses.* New York: Wiley, 1999. All kinds of illusions that will fool your senses, including your sense of smell.

Ripoll, Jaime. *How Your Senses Work.* Broomall, PA: Chelsea House, 1994. Describes how your senses work and how they send messages to your brain.

Simon, Seymour. *Professor I.Q. Explores the Senses.* Starrucca, PA: Dimensions, 1993. Easy-to-do hands-on activities about the senses.

VanCleave, Janice. *Chemistry for Every Kid.* New York: Wiley, 1989. Fun, simple chemistry experiments, including information about perfume.

MORE FUN WITH SMELLS!

Perfume smells because the materials evaporate, and the vapor enters your nose. The alcohol in the perfume evaporates quickly, but the aromatic oils in the perfume remain on your skin and evaporate slowly. You can make a spicy perfume by placing 15 whole cloves in a baby food jar. Fill the jar half full with rubbing alcohol. *CAUTION: Keep alcohol away from your eyes and away from flames.* Secure the lid and allow the jar to sit for 7 days. After that time, use a spoon to stir the contents of the jar, then use your finger to dab a few drops of the alcohol on your wrist. Allow the alcohol to evaporate, then smell your wrist.

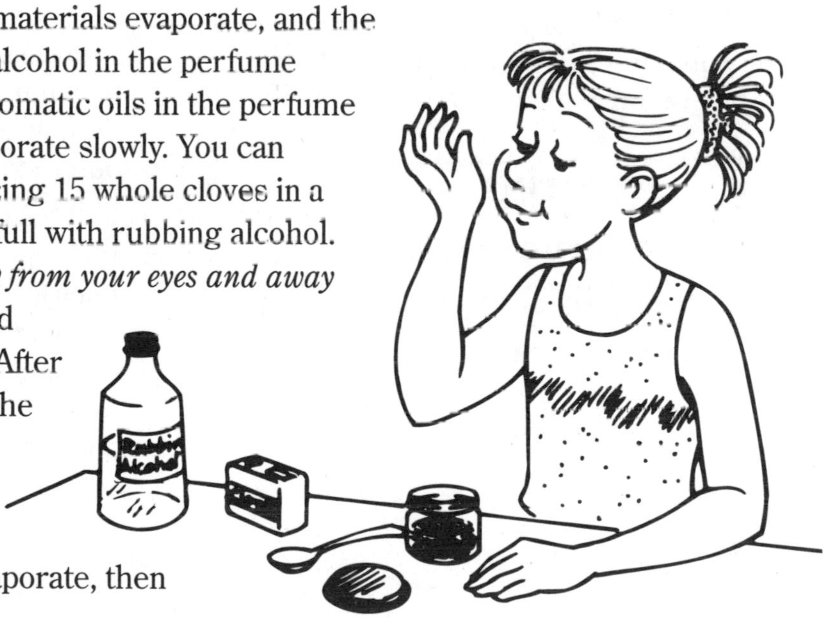

43

Star Locator

DID YOU KNOW?

The star Polaris can tell you where you live!

While Polaris cannot give you your mailing address, its position above the northern horizon can tell you the latitude of where you live. At the equator, Polaris appears at the northern horizon. At the North Pole, it is directly overhead. (Another name for Polaris is the North Star.) In between the equator and the North Pole, the altitude of Polaris above the northern horizon is equal to the observer's latitude north of the equator.

FUN TIME!

Purpose

To measure the approximate altitude of Polaris.

Materials

your hands

Procedure

1. Your hands can be used as a guide to measure the apparent space between the stars or their altitude above the horizon. Practice the hand measurements pictured here.
2. During the day, locate a spot outdoors where you can see the northern horizon. Mark this spot or make a mental note of it.
3. On a clear, moonless night, stand at the marked spot and find the Big Dipper in the northern sky. (For information about the location of the Big Dipper, see chapter 32). Follow an imaginary line from the two outer stars in the bowl of the Big Dipper to Polaris.
4. Use your hands to measure the altitude of Polaris above the horizon. This altitude equals the latitude where you are. For example, if you measure Polaris at four fists above the horizon, this means it is 40° above the horizon, so you are at latitude 40°N.

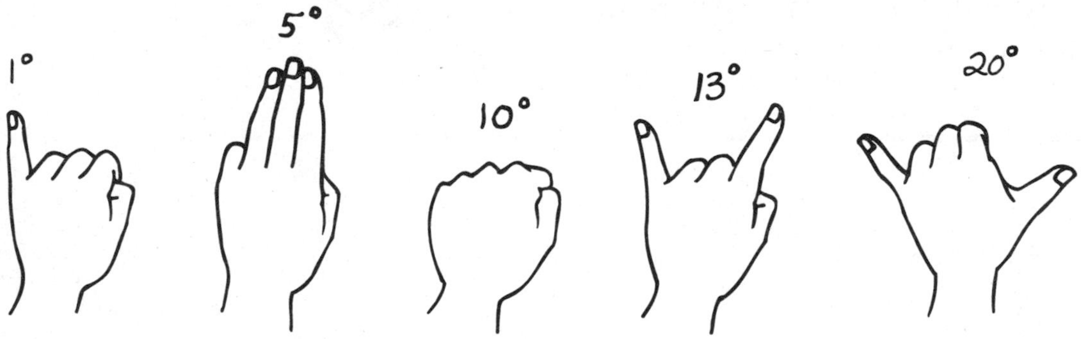

Results

You find Polaris's altitude and your equivalent latitude. Results will vary depending on where you live.

Why?

Because of Polaris's position directly above the North Pole, its altitude in the sky is the same as your latitude on the globe.

BOOK LIST

Levitt, I. M. *Star Maps for Beginners.* New York: Simon & Schuster, 1992. A book of easy-to-follow maps and directions for finding stars and planets. A star map is provided for each month of the year.

Mosely, John. *The Ultimate Guide to the Sky.* Los Angeles: Lowell House, 1997. An easy to use guide containing explanations and descriptions of 88 constellations, and easy-to-read star maps for each month of the year.

VanCleave, Janice. *Astronomy for Every Kid.* New York: Wiley, 1991. Fun, simple astronomy experiments, including information about Polaris and other stars.

———. *Constellations for Every Kid.* New York: Wiley, 1997. Fun, simple constellation experiments, including information about the Big Dipper.

MORE FUN WITH STARS!

Make a flashlight planetarium. Hold a 10-ounce (300-ml) paper cup in one hand. With a pencil, make seven holes in the shape of the Big Dipper in the bottom of the cup. Do this by pushing the pencil point through the cup's bottom from the inside to the outside. Turn on a flashlight and place the bulb end of the flashlight in the open end of the cup. Darken the room and point the bottom of the cup toward the ceiling. The light from the flashlight will shine through the holes and form a star-like pattern of the Big Dipper on the ceiling.

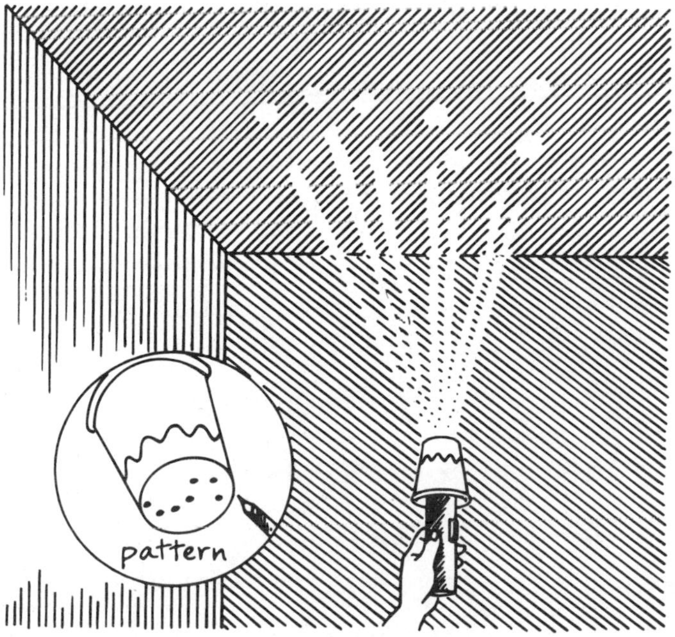

44

Sun Protector

DID YOU KNOW?

Some living things have natural sunscreen!

Sunscreen is a preparation that protects against excessive **ultraviolet light** or **UVL** (invisible light from the Sun that in excess can be dangerous to humans and other forms of life). This protection keeps you from getting a sunburn. Pigments in living things, such as melanin in human skin, are a natural form of protection from UVL. Melanin acts like a light trap that catches UVL, preventing the light from damaging the skin. The less melanin you have, the more your skin can be damaged by UVL. (Freckles are skin areas with extra melanin.)

It is believed that Antarctic **phytoplankton** (small, often microscopic, plant-like creatures that are capable of producing food by using light) may have the capacity to adapt to increased amounts of ultraviolet light by producing their own sunscreen pigments. To help protect your skin from burning by harmful UVL rays, limit your exposure to the Sun, wear protective clothing, and cover your skin with a sunscreen lotion that has a sun protective factor (SPF) of 15 or more.

FUN TIME!

Purpose

To demonstrate how a skin covering protects your skin from the Sun.

Materials

2 sheets of construction paper—1 white, 1 red
one-hole paper punch
4 paper clips
transparent tape

Procedure

1. Fold the white sheet of paper in half twice, placing the long sides together.
2. Use the paper punch to make 30 or more holes in the folded paper.
3. Unfold the paper and place it over the sheet of red paper. Use the paper clips to hold the 2 sheets of paper together.
4. In the middle of the day, lay the papers, white side up, on an outdoor table in the sun. Secure the papers with tape.

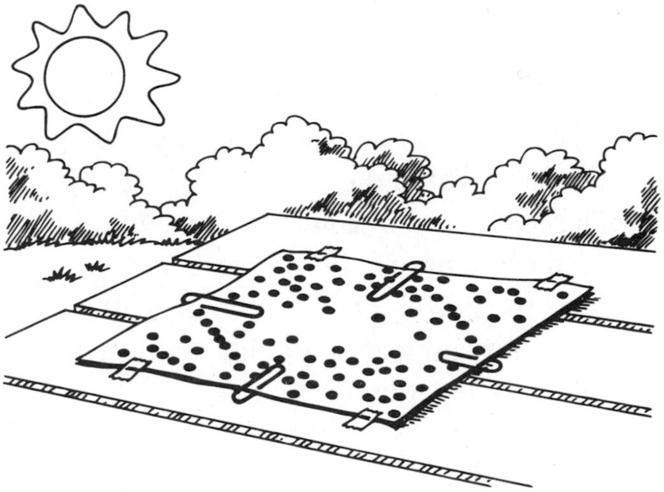

5. After 2 hours or more, remove the papers from the table and separate them. Observe the color of the red paper. *NOTE: It is not necessary to observe the papers during the 2 hours, but if you remain outdoors, wear protective clothing and sunscreen.*

Results

The red paper is covered with pink polka dots.

Why?

As the red pigment combines with oxygen, it fades (gets lighter). This happens naturally over a period of time, but the process is speeded up in the presence of bright sunlight. The white paper, like most of the clothes you wear, is **opaque** (not allowing light to pass through), so it acts as a sunscreen, preventing sunlight from hitting the red paper that it covers. Cutting holes in the paper allowed the sunlight to hit the red paper beneath, causing these areas to fade to pale red to pink polka dots.

BOOK LIST

Kohl, MaryAnn F. *Scribble Art.* Bellingham, WA: Bright Ring, 1994. A collection of art activities, including sun prints.

VanCleave, Janice. *Ecology for Every Kid.* New York: Wiley, 1996. Fun, simple ecology experiments, including information about sunblock.

MORE FUN WITH SUN PRINTS!

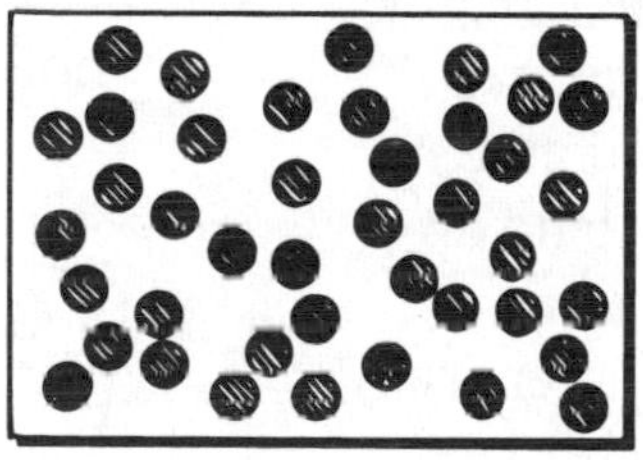

Use sunlight to create animal fur patterns on colored construction paper. To make a cheetah with light spots, use a one-hole paper punch to make holes in a sheet of white paper and place the paper over a sheet of brown paper. Or make a fun red-and-pink striped zebra pattern using red construction paper on the bottom and covering with strips of cover paper to create zebra strips. Set the papers in sunlight, then draw animal shapes on the sun prints and cut them out. The animal cutouts can be glued to craft sticks and used in a puppet show.

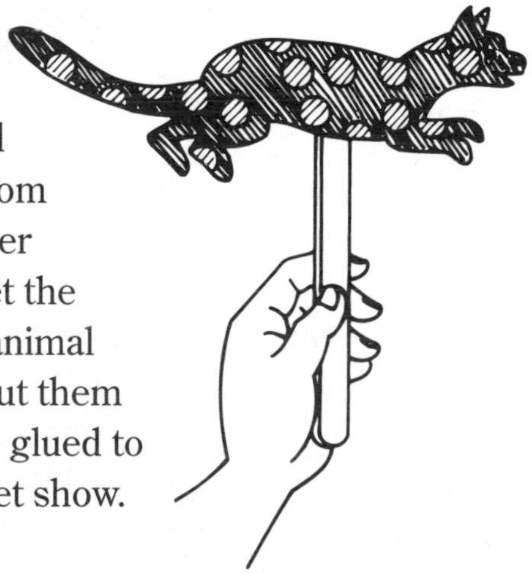

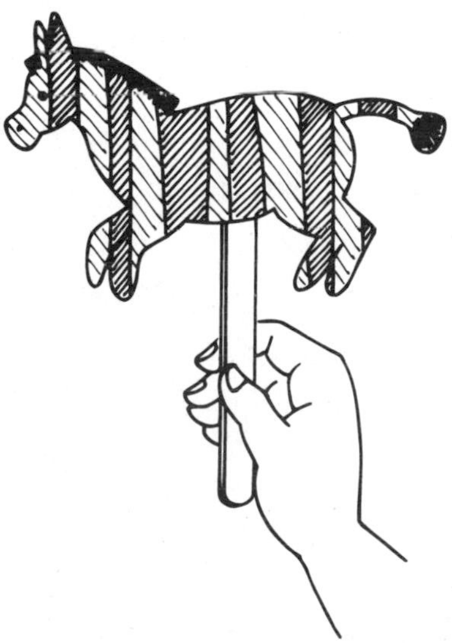

45

Puffy Raisins

DID YOU KNOW?

Grapes are puffed-up raisins!

Even before Native Americans hung strips of buffalo meat in the sun and wind to dry, people dried meats and other foods. They didn't know they were producing an unacceptably dry environment for **microbes** (tiny living things visible only with a microscope, such as bacteria), but they did know it kept their food from spoiling. **Dehydration** (the process of removing water from a material) makes food last longer.

Raisins are made by dehydrating grapes. Before dehydration, grapes are round and puffy. Like all plants, grapes are made up of cells with stiff cell walls. When water is removed from the cells, the walls are generally not changed, but the cells collapse without water to fill them.

FUN TIME!

Purpose

To demonstrate the rehydration of raisins.

Materials

20 raisins
two 10-ounce (300-ml) clear plastic drinking glasses
tap water

Procedure

1. In the morning, place 10 raisins in each glass.
2. Fill one of the glasses with water. Observe the appearance of the raisins in each glass.
3. Allow the glasses to sit undisturbed all day. During this time, observe the raisins in each glass as often as possible. Compare the size and shape of the raisins in each glass.

Results

All the raisins look wrinkled at the start of the experiment. The appearance of the raisins in the glass without water does not change. But the raisins covered with water increase in size, and their shape is more rounded.

Why?

When raisins are placed in water, their cells fill with water and resume their original shape. **Reconstitution** is the process of **rehydrating** (restoring water to) dried food, which means the food is returned to its original **hydrated** (having water) form.

BOOK LIST

Mullane, R. Mike. *Do Your Ears Pop in Space?* New York: Wiley, 1997. Facts about space travel, including information about dehydrated foods.

Pogue, William R. *How Do You Go to the Bathroom in Space?* New York: Tom Doherty, 1991. All the answers to all the questions you have about living in space, including information about dehydrated foods.

VanCleave, Janice. *Nutrition for Every Kid.* New York: Wiley, 1999. Fun, simple nutrition experiments, including information about dehydration.

MORE FUN WITH WATER!

The process by which one substance takes in another, such as a sponge soaking up water, is called **absorption.** Demonstrate absorption by filling a glass about three-fourths full with water. Place a Gummi Bear in the glass. Place a second Gummi Bear in an empty glass. Place the glasses where they will be undisturbed but in view. Observe the bears every hour for 6 hours or more. After the experiment is completed, discard the candy.

46

Up and Out

DID YOU KNOW?

Trees "sweat" huge quantities of water each day!

Trees and other plants don't actually sweat, but they do give off water from their leaves. Water is taken in by the roots of a plant, and the water moves throughout the plant by special transport tubes called **xylem tubes.** In the leaves, the water evaporates and the water vapor moves through **stomata** (small openings in leaves) into the air.

A tree as tall as you are might need at least 10 times as much water per day as you do. Plants need such large amounts of water because they lose up to 98 percent of the water they take in into the air as water vapor. If a plant's roots don't absorb enough water to replace the amount lost, the plant will eventually die from dehydration.

FUN TIME!

Purpose

To demonstrate water loss by plants.

Materials

1-quart (1-liter) plastic bag
tree or bush
transparent tape

Procedure

1. Place the bag over a group of leaves at the end of a stem of an outdoor tree or bush. *NOTE: Do not cut or break the stem off the plant.*
2. Secure the bag to the stem by wrapping tape around the open end of the bag.
3. Observe the contents of the bag as often as possible during the day.

Results

The bag will at first look cloudy, then later water will be seen in the bottom of the bag. The amount of water will vary with the number of leaves in the bag and the type of plant.

Why?

Transpiration is the process by which plants give off vapor through their stomata. This vapor is caught by the plastic bag covering the leaves. Because the plastic is cooler than the air inside the bag, the vapor condenses into water.

BOOK LIST

Dowden, Anne O. *The Blossom on the Bough: A Book of Trees.* Ticknor & Fields, 1994. Discusses the importance of forests, the parts and life cycles of trees, the functions of flowers and fruits, the distinctive features of conifers, and the forest regions in the United States.

Greenaway, Theresa. *DK Pockets: Trees.* New York: Dorling Kindersley, 1995. Which tree is used to make totem poles? Why do leaves change color in autumn? How do trees turn sunlight into food? These and many other questions are answered.

Lawrence, Elanor, and Cecilia Fitzsimons. *An Instant Guide to Trees.* New York: Gramercy Books, 1999. A compact guide to trees commonly seen in gardens, parks, and in the countryside.

VanCleave, Janice. *Plants.* New York: Wiley, 1997. Experiments about transpiration and other plant topics. Each chapter contains ideas that can be turned into award-winning science fair projects.

MORE FUN WITH EVAPORATION!

Nutrients dissolved in water are taken in by a plant's roots. The nutrients remain in the plant when the water leaves the plant. Here is a way to show how dissolved materials are left when water evaporates. Fill a 10-ounce (300-ml) plastic glass half full with tap water. Add 2 tablespoons (30 ml) of salt to the water and stir. Place a sheet of black construction paper on a cookie sheet. Use an artist's paintbrush to write your name or a message on the paper with the salt solution. Stir the salt solution with the brush before making each letter. Ask an adult to heat the oven to 150°F (66°C). Turn the oven off and place the cookie sheet in the oven. Heat the paper for 5 minutes or until it dries. A message will appear as white, shiny crystals on a black background.

47

Dog Days

DID YOU KNOW?

"Dog days" are the hottest days of summer!

In the Northern Hemisphere, the hottest part of summer is generally July and August. During this time, Sirius, a star in the constellation Canis Major, the Great Dog, can be seen rising before sunrise. Sirius, commonly called the Dog Star, is the brightest star in the sky (second only to the Sun). The term "dog days" was coined by the ancient Romans, who believed the heat given off by the Dog Star added to the Sun's heat, thereby causing hot weather.

Sirius is a daytime star in summer and a nighttime star in winter. But the presence of the Dog Star doesn't affect the temperature of summer days any more than it affects the temperature of winter nights.

FUN TIME!

Purpose

To demonstrate how Sirius can be a daytime star in summer and a nighttime star in winter.

Materials

30-inch (75-cm) strip of adding machine paper
marking pen
transparent tape
sheet of unruled white paper
golf ball–size piece of modeling clay
2-inch (5-cm) -diameter circle of yellow construction paper
paper clip

Procedure

1. Lay the strip of adding machine paper on a table.
2. Using the pen, draw a star in the center of the strip. Label the star SIRIUS. Randomly draw unnamed stars along the strip on both sides of Sirius.
3. Overlap and tape the ends of the strip together to form a loop with the stars on the inside.
4. Lay the typing paper on a table and set the loop on the paper.
5. Use the pen to label the paper in front of Sirius WINTER and the paper on the opposite side of the loop SUMMER.
6. Break off a pea-size piece of clay and use it to stand the circle of yellow construction paper in the center of the loop so that one side of the circle faces Sirius. The yellow circle represents the Sun.
7. Mold the remaining clay into a ball and insert the paper clip as shown. The clay ball represents Earth, and the paper clip an observer.
8. Set the clay Earth inside the loop on the winter side of the Sun so that the observer faces Sirius. Is Sirius in the daytime or nighttime sky?
9. Set the clay Earth on the summer side of the Sun so that the observer faces Sirius. Is Sirius in the daytime or nighttime sky?

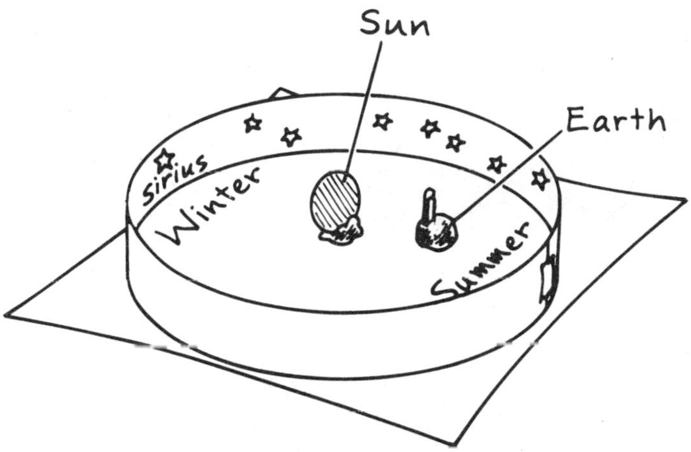

Results

When the clay Earth is in the winter position, the observer faces away from the Sun, so Sirius is in the nighttime sky. In the summer position, the observer faces the Sun, so Sirius is in the daytime sky.

Why?

During winter, Earth is between the Sun and Sirius, so you can see Sirius in the nighttime sky. By summer, Earth has **revolved** (orbited) around the Sun so that the Sun is between Earth and Sirius, and Sirius is in the daytime sky. Because the Sun is so bright, Sirius cannot be seen on summer days.

BOOK LIST

Dickerson, Terence. *Exploring the Night Sky.* Buffalo, NY: Firefly Books, 1989. A user-friendly book for the amateur stargazer.

Heifenz, Milton D., and Will Tirion. *A Walk through the Heavens.* New York: Cambridge University Press, 1998. A guide to stars and constellations and their legends.

VanCleave, Janice. *Constellations for Every Kid.* New York: Wiley, 1997. Fun, simple constellation experiments, including information about Sirius and other stars.

MORE FUN WITH STARS!

Stars are always shining, even in the daytime sky, but the light of the Sun is so bright that light from other stars cannot be seen. Demonstrate this by using a paper punch to make six or more holes in a white index card. Insert the index card in a white envelope. In a lighted room during the daytime, stand with your back to a window and hold the envelope in front of you. The envelope reflects so much light that the lamplight from the room coming through the holes in the card is not visible. Darken the room and turn and face the window. Again, hold the envelope in front of you. The holes in the card are easily seen. Less light is reflected off the envelope, so the background around the holes is dark, making the holes more visible. *CAUTION: Do not look directly at the Sun because the light can permanently damage your eyes.*

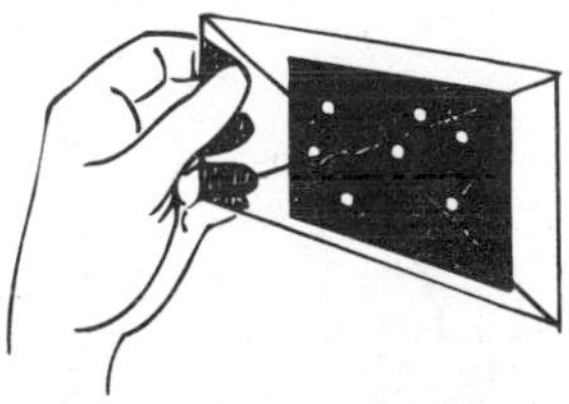

48

Keep Cool

DID YOU KNOW?

A fan does not cool the air!

People use fans, whether electric or hand powered, to cool their bodies, but fans do not cool the air. All they do is make the air move faster. So how do they make you feel cooler on a hot summer day?

What happens is that the moving air blows away the warm air layer above your exposed skin. Your body temperature is about 98.6°F (37°C) and heat from your skin warms the air next to it. When a fan moves this warm air layer away and cooler air takes its place, more heat is then lost from your skin to heat this cooler air. You feel cooler when heat is lost from your skin.

FUN TIME!

Purpose

To demonstrate the cooling effect of moving air.

Materials

you

Procedure

1. Hold the back of your hand close to, but not touching, your mouth.
2. Open your mouth and blow as hard as possible. Observe how warm or cold your breath makes your hand feel.

3. Repeat steps 1 and 2 pursing your lips.

Results

Your hand feels warmer when you blow on it with an open mouth and cooler when you blow on it through pursed lips.

Why?

The temperature of your breath is the same whether your mouth is open or your lips are pursed. The difference in the perceived temperature is that with your mouth open, your warm breath comes out slowly, gently pushes the air layer away above your hand, and takes its place. Since your breath is warmer than the air layer, your skin feels warmer. But when you purse your lips, the air is forced through a smaller opening and comes out of your mouth more rapidly. The faster-moving air not only blows away the air layer above your hand but also blows itself away, allowing cooler air from the room to move in. This makes your skin feel cooler.

BOOK LIST

Carrow, Robert S. *Put a Fan in Your Hat!* New York: McGraw-Hill, 1997. Encourages and fosters the spirit of invention by describing how to build such gadgets as a homemade motor and a hat with a fan in it.

George, Jean Craighead. *One Day in the Desert.* Harper Trophy, 1996. Explains how the animal and human inhabitants of the Sonoran Desert of Arizona adapt and survive the desert's merciless heat.

VanCleave, Janice. *Human Body for Every Kid.* New York: Wiley, 1995. Fun, simple body experiments, including information about keeping the skin cool.

MORE FUN WITH FANS!

Make a paper fan by following these steps. Overlap about ½ inch (1.25 cm) of the short ends of 2 sheets of unruled white paper. Secure the papers to each other with transparent tape. Draw a simple summer scene on one or both sides of the paper. Color the scene with crayons, pens, and/or paints. Starting at one of the shorter ends, make accordion folds about ½ inch (1.25 cm) wide along the length of the paper. Holding one end of the folded paper together, wrap tape around 1 inch (2.5 cm) of the end. This will be the fan's handle. Spread the folded section open and, holding the handle, wave the fan back and forth to cool yourself.

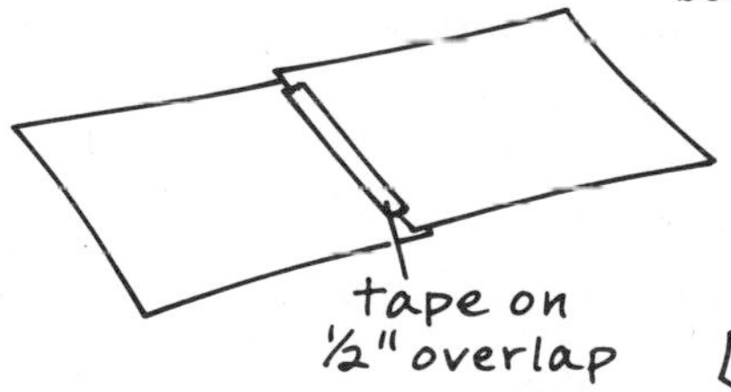

49

Wrinkled Skin

DID YOU KNOW?

Toes and fingers wrinkle when you swim because they absorb water!

The outer layer of skin is made up of layers of flat, dead cells called **squames.** Squames are hexagonal and overlap each other at their edges, like tiles on a roof. Flat layers of squames, plus natural oil called **sebum,** make most of your skin almost waterproof. But the skin on your fingers and toes is not waterproof. This skin has many more layers of squames than other parts of your body, but it lacks the **glands** (organs that produce a fluid which the body can use) that make sebum. Because of its thickness and lack of water resistance, the skin on your fingers and toes soaks up many times as much water as other skin layers when you stay in water a long time. The swollen squames are too big to lie flat, so the skin wrinkles.

FUN TIME!

Purpose

To demonstrate why fingers and toes wrinkle in water.

Materials

scissors
ruler
new cellulose kitchen sponge
bowl of tap water
petroleum jelly

Procedure

1. Cut a 1-inch (2.5-cm) -wide strip from the sponge. Keep the strip.
2. Cut a section from the sponge strip so that about half the strip is half as thick.
3. Put the strip in the bowl of water until it's soaked, then take it out and squeeze out as much water as possible. Allow the sponge to dry thoroughly. This may take several hours.
4. Press the dry sponge strip with your fingers, making it as flat as possible.
5. Thoroughly coat the surface of the thinner section of the sponge strip with petroleum jelly.
6. Dip your finger in the water in the bowl and hold your wet finger above the part of the sponge coated with petroleum jelly. Allow 2 to 3 water drops to fall onto the sponge. Observe the surface of the sponge.

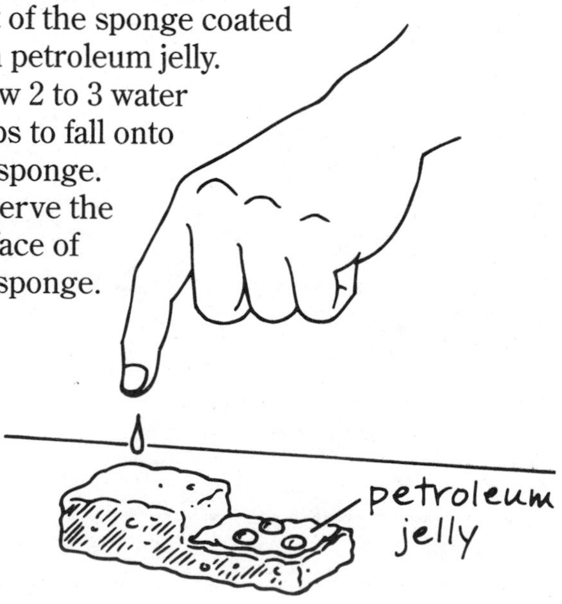

7. Repeat step 6 dropping water onto the uncoated, thicker part of the sponge.

Results

The uncoated part of the sponge absorbs water and wrinkles.

Why?

The skin on the tips of your fingers and toes is different from the rest of your skin. It is thicker, and like the uncoated part of the sponge, it is not waterproofed with a coating of oil. That's why it soaks up water and wrinkles when you have been in water for a long time.

BOOK LIST

Allison, Linda. *Blood and Guts.* New York: Little, Brown and Company, 1976. Helps you explore the amazing bag you live in, your skin and the parts inside.

Savage, Stephen. *Skin.* Boston: Thomson Learning, 1995. Describes the body coverings of humans and other animals, explaining the varying uses of skin, fur, feathers, spines, scales, and hair.

VanCleave, Janice. *Human Body for Every Kid.* New York: Wiley, 1995. Fun, simple body experiments, including information about skin wrinkling.

MORE FUN WITH WRINKLES!

Moist air can make hair twist and bend. Here's a way to see how water changes the shape of some hair. Stand a paper-wrapped straw on a table and push the paper wrapper down around the straw until the wrapper is as squashed as possible. Take the squashed, wrinkled wrapper off the straw and put it on a table. Fill a cup half full with water. Dip your finger in the water. Use your finger to put a drop of water on a section of the wrapper. Dip your finger in the water again and put a drop of water on another section of the wrapper. Watch the wrinkled wrapper twist and bend.

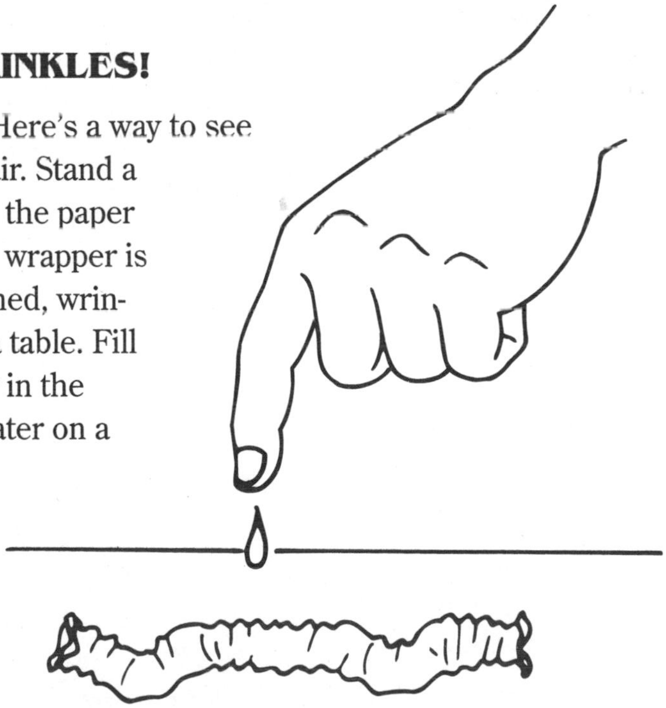

50

Singing Lessons

DID YOU KNOW?

Birds learn their songs!

Birds are born with the ability to sing, but they learn the songs of their species. If a baby bird is isolated from other birds of its species, it can sing simple songs, because this ability is inherited, but not the more complex songs of its species. These it must hear and learn. Most birds can only sing the songs of their species. But some birds, such as parrots and mynahs in captivity, imitate human speech and other sounds. The mockingbird seems to be the best at imitating the songs of other birds. It too has to have heard the songs of other birds to learn them.

FUN TIME!

Purpose

To discover how birds sing.

Materials

9-inch (23-cm) round balloon

Procedure

1. Inflate the balloon, then hold the neck of the balloon between the first fingers and thumbs of both hands.
2. Slowly stretch the neck of the balloon sideways as far as possible, making a narrow opening that lets the air out slowly. Observe the sound produced.
3. Repeat step 3 moving the neck of the balloon back and forth to produce different sounds.

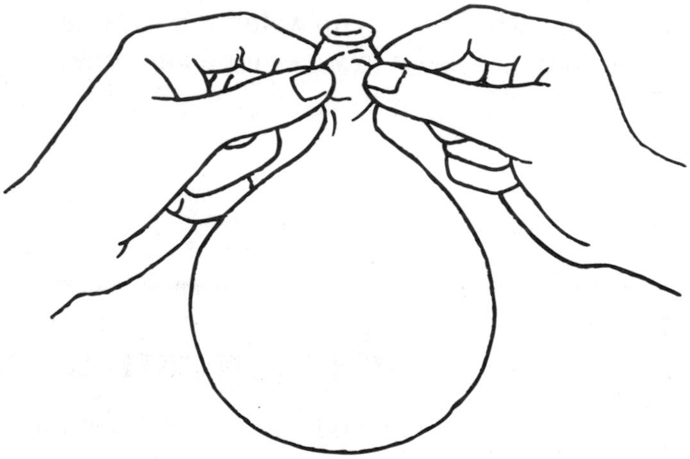

Results

The sound changed when you changed the shape of the balloon's opening.

Why?

Birds have a **syrinx** (sound-producing organ in birds) in their **windpipe** (a tube to the lungs through which air passes in and out of the body). The number of muscles around the syrinx determines the type of sound produced. In general, the more muscles, the wider variety of notes a bird can sing.

The syrinx is located where the windpipe divides into two tubes, one going to each lung, so birds can produce two notes at once. The human **larynx** or **voice box** (sound-producing organ) does not divide, so humans can produce only one note at a time. The larynx has **vocal cords** (two strips of tough, elastic muscle stretched across the opening of the larynx) and the syrinx has tympanic membranes that vibrate when air passes across them. As the syrinx changes in size due to the **contraction** (shortening) of muscles around it, different sounds are produced. Like the tympanic membranes of a bird's syrinx, the balloon vibrated and produced different sounds as the size of the opening changed. The faster the opening vibrated, the higher the pitch of the sound produced.

BOOK LIST

Arnosky, Jim. *Bird Watcher.* New York: Random House, 1997. Briefly presents tips on bird-watching and provides blank pages for keeping records of sightings and sounds.

Harrison, George H. *Backyard Bird Watching for Kids.* Minocqua, WI: Willow Creek Press, 1997. Provides ideas for interacting with nature while learning about the needs and behaviors of birds.

Hill, Elizabeth Starr. *Bird Boy.* New York: Farrar Straus, 1999. Chang, a Chinese boy mute from birth but able to imitate bird sounds, is thrilled when his father, a cormorant fisherman, decides he's old enough to help with the "Big Catch." Chang does so well that he is then allowed to help raise a coromorant chick. When a local bully, Jinan, steals it, Chang must stand up for himself and rescue the bird.

VanCleave, Janice. *Animals.* New York: Wiley, 1993. Experiments about birds and other animals. Each chapter contains ideas that can be turned into award-winning science fair projects.

MORE FUN WITH BIRDSONGS!

Chickens have a simple syrinx, so they make a few sounds, but don't sing. A chicken's clucking sounds are produced by a vibrating tympanic membrane. You can produce similar sounds by vibrating a string. Make a clucking chicken using these steps. Punch a hole in the bottom of a 9-ounce (270-ml) paper cup. Thread a 12-inch (30-cm) string through the hole and tie one end of the string to a paper clip on the outside of the cup. Tie the other end of the string around a small rectangular piece of kitchen sponge. Wet the sponge with water. Wrap the wet sponge around the string near the opening of the cup. Squeeze the sponge against the string as you move the sponge toward you along the string in jerky movements. It may take a little practice to produce clucking chicken sounds.

51

Cool Clothes

DID YOU KNOW?

Pale colors are cool!

The Sun is the closest star to Earth, at a distance of only about 93 million miles (143 million km). The next closest star is about 300,000 times farther away. The Sun, like all stars, is a ball of hot, glowing gases. **Solar energy** is energy from the Sun and includes heat rays, visible light, and ultraviolet light. The solar energy that reaches Earth warms its surface and the air around Earth, as well as objects on the surface, including you.

The color of Earth's surface, and of objects on it, affects their temperature. Darker-colored objects get hotter than do pale-colored objects because they absorb more solar energy. Light-colored objects reflect it. This is why you will feel cooler in the summertime when you wear pale-colored clothes.

FUN TIME!

Purpose

To demonstrate how the color of clothes affects temperature.

Materials

2 outdoor thermometers
pen or pencil
paper
ruler
2 cotton T-shirts—1 black, 1 white
timer

Procedure

1. Read and record the temperature on each thermometer.
2. In a sunny outdoor area, place the thermometers about 24 inches (60 cm) apart on a table.
3. Lay one shirt on top of each thermometer. Smooth the shirts so they press against the thermometers.
4. After 10 minutes, read and record the temperature on each thermometer.

Results

The temperature reading of the thermometer under the dark shirt is higher than that of the thermometer under the pale shirt.

Why?

The dark cloth absorbs more solar energy than the white cloth. The white cloth reflects more of the energy. The absorption of solar energy raises the temperature of the material.

BOOK LIST

Daley, Michael. *Amazing Sun Fun Activities.* New York: McGraw-Hill, 1997. Provides an introduction to solar energy through hands-on experiments.

Hillerman, Anne. *Done in the Sun.* Santa Fe, NM: Sunstone Press, 1983. An introduction to the Sun as a renewable energy source, demonstrating through simple experiments and craft projects how the Sun's light and heat can help us in our everyday lives.

VanCleave, Janice. *Ecology for Every Kid.* New York: Wiley, 1996. Fun, simple ecology experiments, including information about solar energy.

MORE FUN WITH THE SUN!

Solar energy can be used to prepare food. Prepare sun tea by following these steps. Fill a clean 1-quart (1-liter) jar with tap water. Add 2 tea bags to the jar and close the jar. After about 10:00 A.M., place the jar outside in direct sunlight. Observe the jar every hour for 2 hours or more. When you think the sun tea is as strong as you like, open the jar and discard the tea bags. Sweeten the tea to your desired taste and add ice. Voilà! You have ice-cold sun tea to cool you on a summer day.

52

Sweaty Cans

DID YOU KNOW?

Soda cans don't sweat!

On warm, humid summer days, the outside of a cold soda can or a glass containing an iced drink becomes covered with liquid. Some people might think the can or glass is leaking, and some might say it is sweating. But neither explanation is correct. Instead, water vapor in the air is collecting on the containers. Water can exist in three forms, gas (vapor), liquid, and solid (ice). It takes a change of energy for water to change from one form to another. The gas form contains the most energy and the solid the least. So to condense, to change from a gas to a liquid, requires a loss of energy. When water vapor in the air comes in contact with a cold surface, like the outside of a soda can, the gas condenses. It loses energy and changes into a liquid. As more and more liquid forms, the outside of the can becomes covered with a film of liquid water.

FUN TIME!

Purpose

To demonstrate condensation.

Materials

drinking glass
ice
tap water

Procedure

1. Fill the glass with ice.
2. Add water to the glass until filled.
3. Set the glass on a table and observe its outside surface as often as possible for 5 minutes or more.

Results

Water drops form on the outside surface of the glass.

Why?

Molecules of water vapor have more energy than liquid water, so they move around more quickly. When the gas molecules come in contact with the cold surface of the glass, they lose energy and slow down. As this happens, the separate molecules group together and bond (join together), forming chains of water molecules. The combined molecules collect, forming a layer of visible liquid water on the glass's surface.

BOOK LIST

Galastic, Alex. *Dudley's Tea Party.* New York: Scholastic Trade, 1995. Dudley the dragon throws a tea party, and has to solve the mystery of why the water is all dried up.

Hooper, Meredith, and Christopher Coady. *The Drop in My Drink.* New York: Viking Children's Press, 1998. The story of water on our planet. Includes a detailed depiction of the water cycle, amazing facts about water, plus important environmental information.

VanCleave, Janice. *Chemistry for Every Kid.* New York: Wiley, 1989. Fun, simple chemistry experiments, including information about evaporation.

MORE FUN WITH WATER!

In a glass of water, a water molecule on the water's surface has other water molecules on all sides except above it. If this molecule has enough energy, it can move fast enough to break away and escape as vapor into the air above it. This process of changing from a liquid to a gas is called evaporation. Make a water painting that evaporates. Fill a bucket or bowl with tap water. Using a 2-inch (5-cm) or wider paintbrush, dip the brush in the water and paint designs on outdoor surfaces, such as a sidewalk or building. How long does your work of art last in the summer sun?

Glossary

abscission layer The layer of cells holding the petiole of a leaf to the stem.

absorb To take in.

absorption The process by which one substance takes in another, such as a sponge soaking up water.

accretion The process by which cloud droplets bump into each other and combine to form raindrops.

altitude Angular height above the horizon.

altostratus clouds Flat, layered clouds that occur at high altitudes.

amphibians Animals, such as frogs, toads, and salamanders, that are cold-blooded, live part of their lives in water and the other on land, and do not have hair, scales, or feathers.

amylase A chemical in saliva that digests starch.

anole A reptile that is closely related to the chameleon.

Antarctic Circle Latitude 66.50°S.

Antarctic region The region of Earth south of the Antarctic Circle.

anthocyanins Red to purple pigments in plants.

Arctic Circle Latitude 66.50°N.

Arctic region The region of Earth north of the Arctic Circle.

arteries Blood vessels that carry blood away from the heart.

asterism A group of stars that form a shape within a constellation, such as the Big Dipper in the constellation Ursa Major.

atmosphere The blanket of air around Earth.

astronomers Scientists who study celestial bodies.

atoms The building blocks of all substances.

autumnal equinox The first day of autumn, on or about September 23 in the Northern Hemisphere and on or about March 21 in the Southern Hemisphere, when day and night are of equal length.

axis An imaginary line running through Earth perpendicular to the equator.

bilateral symmetry Symmetry in which the two halves of a figure are mirror images of each other.

bile A juice made by the liver that breaks fats into tiny globules that can then be digested and used to make energy.

blade The broad part of a leaf.

blood vessels Tubes through which blood flows.

blubber An extra-thick layer of insulating fat under the skin of some animals, such as penguins.

carnivore A meat eater.

carotene A yellow or orange pigment in living things.

celestial bodies Natural objects in the sky, such as stars, the Moon, and the Sun.

celestial poles Points in the sky above the North Pole and South Pole of Earth.

cells The basic building blocks of all living things.

chlorophyll A green pigment found in plants.

chromatophore A skin cell containing pigments.

circumpolar stars Stars that do not rise or set, but stay above the horizon as they circle a celestial pole.

cirrus clouds White, wispy clouds made of ice crystals that occur at high altitudes.

cold-blooded Having a body temperature that changes with the temperature of the surroundings.

concentration For a liquid solution it is a measure of the amount of dissolved particles in a liquid.

condense To change from a vapor to a liquid.

constellation A group of stars that appears to make a pattern in the sky.

contraction Shortening.

crystal A solid material with flat surfaces that has particles arranged in repeating patterns.

daylight saving time (DST) A time when clocks are set forward 1 hour so that there are more usable hours of daylight in the evening. In the United States, this is the time between the first Sunday in April and the last Sunday in October.

deciduous Having leaves that are lost in autumn.

dehydration The process of removing water from a material.

density A measure of the mass of a given volume of a material.

diffract To bend light around an object.

digest To break down a substance physically or by a chemical change, and in animals and some plants, to break down the substance into simple nutrients that can be used by the animal's or plant's body cells.

dilate To get bigger.

dissolve To break into small particles and mix thoroughly with a liquid.

effort force The force applied to a lever.

electrons Negatively charged particles spinning outside the nucleus of an atom.

emulsifier A substance that prevents an emulsion from separating.

emulsion A mixture of two liquids that do not dissolve in each other, such as oil and water.

equator An imaginary line around Earth at 0° latitude.

evaporate To change from a liquid to a vapor.

fasts Doesn't eat.

fat A nutrient, insulator, and protective cushioning in the body of animals.

first-class lever A lever in which the fulcrum is between the effort and resistance forces.

freeze To change from a liquid to a solid due to a decrease in temperature.

freezing point The temperature at which a substance freezes.

friction A force that tends to stop the motion of objects that are moving against each other.

fulcrum The fixed point on which a lever rotates.

gland An organ that produces a fluid which the body can use.

glide To fly without flapping the wings, as butterflies and other flying creatures sometimes do.

glycopeptide A sugar-like substance in some creatures, such as fish, that helps to keep ice from forming inside the creature.

gravity The force that pulls things toward the center of Earth.

habitat The natural surroundings of living things.

halo A white or faintly colored ring around the Moon.

hexagonal Having a six-sided structure.

hibernate To live in a sleep-like condition of partial or total inactivity.

hormones Chemicals that affect behavior in plants and animals.

humidity The amount of moisture in the air.

hydrated Having water.

hygrometer An instrument that measures humidity.

hygroscopic Absorbing water from the air.

ice crystals Crystals that form when water freezes.

illuminate To light up.

incinerator A furnace for burning trash.

insulate To reduce the movement of heat energy into or out of a material.

insulator A material that insulates.

iridescent Having shiny rainbow-like coloring.

krill Small shrimp-like animals.

landfill A low area that is built up from deposits of solid trash.

larynx The sound-producing organ in humans.

latitude Angular distance north or south of the equator.

lever A type of machine such as a bar, board, or straight stick that rotates about a fulcrum.

liquid solution A mixture of a liquid, such as water, and dissolved particles of another substance, such as salt.

liver An organ in vertebrates that produces bile.

load The object moved by a machine such as a lever.

longitude Angular distance east or west of the prime meridian.

lunar corona A crown of colors around the Moon caused by diffraction of water in Earth's atmosphere.

magnetic north pole The northernmost place on Earth to which a compass needle points.

mass An amount of material.

matter What all stuff is made of.

melanin A dark brown pigment that gives skin color.

meteorologist A scientist who studies the weather.

microbe Tiny living things visible only with a microscope, such as bacteria.

migrate To move seasonally from one region to another, often covering great distances.

molecule A particle made of two or more atoms.

nectar A sugary liquid in flowers.

nerves Bundles of cells that send messages throughout the body.

netted Branched, as in the large veins of a leaf.

night blindness An inability to see well at night due to a lack of visual purple in the eye.

Northern Hemisphere The region of Earth north of the equator.

North Pole The north end of Earth's axis; true north.

nucleus The center of an atom, containing protons.

nurseryman A person who grows and sells plants.

nutrients Materials needed by living things for growth, energy, and good health.

odor The property of a substance that activates the smell detectors in the nose.

oil Liquid fat.

opaque Not allowing light to pass through.

orbit To move in a curved path around another body; the curved path of one body moving around another.

organ A part of a living thing that performs a special job, such as the heart, liver, or glands.

ovipositor The egg-laying tube of an insect.

palmate Having a netted vein pattern in which all of the veins start at the petiole and extend through the blade like fingers on the palm of a hand.

palmate leaflets Separate smaller leaves that radiate from a common point at the petiole of a leaf.

parallel Running in the same direction, as in the large veins of a leaf.

petiole The stalk of a leaf.

photosensitive pigments Pigments in the retina of the eye that detect light.

phytoplankton Small, often microscopic, plant-like creatures that are capable of producing food by using light.

pigment A substance that gives a material color by absorbing, reflecting, and transmitting visible light.

pinnate Having a netted vein pattern in which a single large vein runs through the center of the leaf and smaller veins branch from it like a feather.

pinnate leaflets Separate smaller leaves that are attached along a central petiole of a leaf.

pitch The high or low quality of a sound.

Polaris The North Star.

prime meridian An imaginary line around Earth at 0° longitude.

proboscis The feeding tube of some insects, such as flies and butterflies.

protons Positively charged particles in the nucleus of an atom.

pulp A soft, moist, slightly sticky material made from ground-up wood that is used to make paper.

pulse The stretching of blood vessels corresponding to the heartbeat.

pupil The black dot-like opening in the center of the eye.

radial symmetry Symmetry in which all parts of a figure spread out from the center like the spokes of a wheel.

reconstitution The process of rehydrating a material such as dried food.

reflect To throw back or bounce off of, as light reflected by or onto a surface.

rehydrate To restore water to a material.

reptile A cold-blooded vertebrate that breathes with lungs and has dry, scaly, or horny skin.

resistance force The force a lever applies on a load.

retina The inner, light-sensitive lining at the back of the eyeball.

revolve To orbit a body.

saliva A liquid containing chemicals that digest some foods.

sap A watery liquid in plants that contains nutrients.

sapling A small tree.

sebum Natural oil in skin.

second-class lever A lever in which the resistance force is between the effort force and the fulcrum.

shivering The trembling of muscles.

sleet Frozen raindrops.

snow Snowflakes that fall and collect on the ground.

snow crystal A crystal of frozen water made by the sublimation of water vapor.

snowflake A collection of colliding snow crystals.

solar energy Energy from the Sun, including heat rays, visible light, and ultraviolet light.

sound waves Vibrations traveling through air or another material.

Southern Hemisphere The region of Earth south of the equator.

South Pole The south end of the Earth's axis.

species A specific type of living thing.

spectroscope An instrument used by astronomers to separate starlight into a spectrum.

spectrum A band of colors seen when a beam of light passes through a material that separates the light rays.

squames Flat, dead cells occurring in layers in the outer layer of skin.

stable In chemicals, the quality of not easily being broken down.

starch A complex chemical found in many foods.

static charges Stationary electric charges in static electricity.

static electricity A buildup of electric charges.

stomata Small openings in leaves through which vapor can pass.

stridulation Process of producing sound by rubbing one body part against another, as crickets do.

sublimation The process by which a vapor changes to a solid or a solid to a vapor without becoming a liquid.

summer solstice The first day of summer, on or about June 21 in the Northern Hemisphere and on or about December 22 in the Southern Hemisphere, and the longest day of the year.

sunscreen A preparation that protects against excessive UV radiation.

superstition A belief not based on knowledge.

surface tension The tendency of molecules of a liquid to cling together at the surface, forming a skin-like film.

syrinx The sound-producing organ in birds.

third-class lever A lever in which the effort force is between the fulcrum and the resistance force.

transmit To pass through, as light transmitted through pigment.

transpiration The process by which plants give off vapor through their stomata.

true north The direction of the North Pole.

turgor movement Plant movement due to turgor pressure.

turgor pressure Pressure caused by water inside a plant cell.

tympanic membrane A thin, flexible skin that vibrates in response to sound waves.

utlraviolet light (UVL) Invisible light from the Sun that in excess can be dangerous to humans or other forms of life.

vapor Gas.

vaporize To change to a vapor.

veins A network of tubes in a leaf that support the blade and conduct sap.

vernal equinox The first day of spring, on or about March 21 in the Northern Hemisphere and on or about September 23 in the Southern Hemisphere, when day and night are of equal length.

vertebrate An animal with a backbone.

vibrate To move quickly back and forth.

visual purple The main photosensitive pigment in the eye.

vocal cords Two strips of tough, elastic muscle stretched across the opening of the larynx.

voice box See larynx.

volume The amount of space that a material occupies.

water cycle The evaporation of water from Earth and the return of that water either in solid or liquid form.

waterspout A tornado that touches down on water instead of land.

Western Hemisphere The region of Earth consisting mainly of North and South America.

white light Visible light that is made up of all the rainbow colors of light.

wind Air in horizontal motion.

windpipe A tube to the lungs through which air passes into and out of the body.

wind sock A tapered cloth tube used to indicate wind direction and intensity.

winter solstice The first day of winter, on or about December 22 in the Northern Hemisphere and on or about June 21 in the Southern Hemisphere, and the shortest day of the year.

xylem tubes Tubes in plants that carry water from the roots throughout the plant.

zenith A point in the sky directly overhead.

Index